Application of Six Sigma in Library and Information Science

Application of Six Sigma in Library and Information Science

Editors:
Vrushali Dandavate
Ajay Khatri
Pradip Umdale

Ess Ess Publications
New Delhi

Application of Six Sigma in Library and Information Science

ISBN: 978-81-7000-685-5

Rs.775/-

First Published 2013

Published by:
Ess Ess Publications
4831/24, Ansari Road,
Darya Ganj,
New Delhi-110 002.
INDIA
Phones: 23260807, 41563444
Fax: 41563334
E-mail: info@essessreference.com
www.essessreference.com

Cover Design by *Patch Creative Unit*

Printed and bound in India at Salasar Imaging Systems.

Contents

APPLICATION OF INFORMATION TECHNOLOGY ON LIBRARY SERVICES

LIBRARY MANAGEMENT

Preface

The eventual goal of any library is users satisfaction. Six sigma help us to do continues appraisal and improve the quality of the library to satisfy the library users in an effective and better manner. Six Sigma will improve the quality of the library, maximizing the users satisfaction and promote better performance.

One day national conference on 'Application of Six Sigma in Library Science Field' provides on opportunities for researchers and experts to meet and exchange research results, innovative ideas and state-of-the-art developments in library and information science.

The theme of the conference, 'Application of Six sigma in Library Science' reflects importance of the standardization is increasing in number of field library is one of them. Many libraries are going for ISO standardization also. This conference will be helpful for librarians to face and cope up with standardization process. According to six sigma, defects include all causes that interrupt process or service. It is a methodology to define a problem from the view point of managers or users as a defect and ascertain its causes in order to solve it. As a theory it was originally used in manufacturing. Today it applies to service areas including library. The purpose of this conference is to search for applications of six sigma as a solution for efficient knowledge management. It also aims to establish information infrastructure and secure service competitiveness, and finally to improve user satisfaction, the ultimate goal of libraries.

We also acknowledge the sponsors, program committee members, conference support committees, and individuals who gave their continuous help and support in making the conference a success. We fervently hope that the conference will continue to grow from strength to strength travels to different Institutes in India, and will continue to provide a stimulating and enriching platform for innovative ideas, to enable us to design and developed new concepts of managements and Information technologies in Library and Information Science.

We would like to thank all the authors who contributed their papers to the conference, We would also like to thank members of Six Sigma conference Organizing Committee, Finally we want to express worm thanks to the Management of AISSMS and to our Principal Dr S P Danao for their enthusiasm and constructive way of cooperation.

There are many other people who played equally critical roles, either as member or non-members of the committees; it is difficult to mention them by individual names, we appreciate their every effort to make this event a success. Finally Ess Ess Publications, New Delhi, deserves our heartfelt thanks for printing this book.

— EDITORS

1

Six Sigma and Its Application in Library Services

Ms. Divya Chaudhary

JRF Central Library, Ch. Charan Singh University, Meerut

Dr. Shiva Kanaujia Sukula

Asstt. Librarian, Central Library, Ch. Charan Singh University, Meerut

ABSTRACT

A fundamental objective of six sigma is to achieve customer satisfaction. Doing things right and keeping them consistent are the ideas behind six sigma. Success of six sigma in manufacturing is well published. But the same cannot be said about its implementation in services. Applying six sigma to services is still limited. This paper deals with the concept of Six Sigma. It highlights the advantages of six sigma. It explains Quality management in libraries by implementing six sigma application. It provides Six Sigma Approach to Continuous Improvement. . It also provides Application of Six Sigma in Services Sector. It explains the future of six sigma.

Keywords: Six sigma, Quality management in libraries, Advantage of six sigma,

INTRODUCTION

A transformation is needed for libraries from focusing on the traditional information provider in the service operation system to focusing on the information recipient, that is, the customer. In particular, libraries are faced with radically changing user demands as well as environment changes. Thus new management strategies and techniques are required for libraries. Knowledge management as a process can facilitate innovation for the library to acquire and store information and knowledge in the organization either internally or externally, to create and share knowledge, and to utilize, accumulate and reuse such knowledge. In short, knowledge management is a series of processes of the knowledge transformation and circulation. It should be regarded as the highest priority that the user is the center of all the processes from the initial phase of service planning to the final phase of evaluation, so the changing needs of the user are met and new ones are created. Along with consideration of the user priority, it is also important to secure a sufficient amount of information for decision making and to define and comprehend the cause based on the statistical analysis of this information. Moreover, it is essential to clarify knowledge elements relevant to the future core capacity, comparing it with the standard of the current organization and restructuring based on the result.[1] The eventual goal of any library is "users' satisfaction". Through implementing Six Sigma user can do continues appraisal and can full fill users' needs.[2] Since the introduction of six sigma in the 1980s, there have been many success stories from companies like Motorola, General Electric, and Allied Signal. The majority of these stories are from the manufacturing sector. The service sector, barring the health care and banking industries, are lagging behind in applying and reaping the benefits of six sigma. While quality management tools have existed for a long time, their use is still not widely implemented in services. The emergence of six sigma has renewed interest in the scientific management of service industries. The basic elements of six sigma are really not new.

Statistical process control, failure mode and effect analysis, cause and effect diagram, and other tools have been in use for some time. Six sigma offers a framework that unites these basic quality tools with high level management support.[3]

WHAT IS SIX SIGMA?

The Six Sigma approach identifies and eliminates defects with a structured, data-driven, problem-solving method of using rigorous data-gathering and statistical analysis. The statistical representation of Six Sigma describes quantitatively how a process is performing. To achieve Six Sigma, a process must not produce more than 3.4 defects per million opportunities. A Six Sigma defect is defined as anything outside of user specifications. Six Sigma differs from traditional quality improvement programs in its focus on input variables. While traditional process improvement methods depend upon measuring outputs and establishing control plans to shield customers from organizational defects, a Six Sigma program demands that problems be addressed at the input root cause level, thereby eliminating the need for unnecessary inspection and rework processes.[4]

QUALITY MANAGEMENT IN LIBRARIES

Generally libraries are giving much attention on quality service to focus on users satisfaction. Quality service can be delivered if libraries improve its management efficiency. In general readymade service will help to satisfy users. Readymade service can be efficiently done through the process of Sig Sigma. First define the demand of the users then measure it, analyze the same, make in control and improve the quality then serve to users. Library is a place where enormous of information is acquired, stored, classified and disseminated to its users at the maximum to satisfy their needs. To achieve this task library should have quality management process in libraries. So we have define the actual needs of the library users' by focusing on their demands, measure, analyze, and control over it.[5]

SIX SIGMA APPROACH TO CONTINUOUS IMPROVEMENT

Six Sigma is traditionally a mechanism for reducing defects during the discrete manufacturing through the use of analytical methods and statistics. It is a highly refined, data intensive approach to problem solving. Six Sigma was developed by Motorola in 1986. It is a business management strategy. It is widely used in many areas of library. Six Sigma is a set of practices designed to improve manufacturing processes and to eliminate defects. It works with highly complex design and process problems or problems that are enterprise wide.

APPLICATION OF SIX SIGMA IN SERVICES SECTOR

Just as for manufacturing, defects found in service incur a cost to either scrap or to rework. Examples include the need to re-contact a user to verify an order, providing an incorrect service, providing a substandard service or even over service or providing more than what is required. Service organizations such as healthcare and finance have been implementing six sigma and are registering benefits. The breadth of applications is now expanding to other services including call centers and human resource and product support services. Literature review shows that most applications are limited to service industries in North America and the European countries, but it is the financial benefits of six sigma that have been publicized, instead of discussing gain in terms of process improvement. Also, important to note is that the applications emphasized the proper identification of critical success factors (CSFs), CTQ characteristics, and key performance indicators (KPIs).

SIX SIGMA FOR SOFTWARE QUALITY ASSURANCE

Nevertheless, there were only occasionally attempts to implement Six Sigma for software. Applying Six Sigma to software development makes product development and other projects transparent to both management and user. However, transparency requires an important cultural change. Users know from experience that bad communication is a major reason why projects fail, and software projects in particular. User expects from better transparency that meeting both deadlines and user requirements becomes easier. The major problem with early Six Sigma attempts was that there was no connection of software metrics to economic success. Counting mistakes and defects is not a clear indication if the software project is going to be successful. Other metrics like time-to-market and user friendliness are much more important in many application areas. Sometimes, reliability is of essence, but not always. There is no software metrics that serves all. It depends what kind of software user are developing or installing. Finding good metrics for software development or deployment is a major task in itself.

FUTURE OF SIX SIGMA

Six sigma is likely to remain as one of the key initiatives to improve the management process than just being remembered as one of the fads. The primary focus should be on improving overall management performance, not just pinpointing and counting defects. Researchers and practitioners are trying to integrate six sigma with other existing innovative management practices that have been around to make six sigma method even more attractive to different organizations that might have not started or fully implemented the six sigma method. Integrating and comparing principles and characteristics of six sigma with Total Quality Management. Human Resource Functions, Lean Production ,ISO 9000, ISO 9001, and the capability maturity model are all part of the quality community's effort to maximize the positive effect of the six sigma method.

REFERENCE:

1. A Study on Introducing Six Sigma Theory in the Library for Service Competitiveness Enhancement http://archive.ifla.org/IV/ifla72/papers/146-Kim-en.pdf
2. Six Sigma in Libraries : A Management Perspective http://www.ampublisher.com

3. The Extent of Six Sigma Methodologies Usage in Services http://www.iamot.org/conference/index.php/ocs/9/paper/download/1766/806

4. What is Six Sigma? http://www.ssqi.com/six-sigma-library/index.html http://librariansinfo.blogspot.com/2011/03/application-of--six-sigma-concept-to.html

5. Application of Six sigma concept to Effective Academic Library Management and users Satisfaction

6. Advantages and Disadvantages of Six Sigma http://www.sixsigma.in/advantages-and- disadvantages-of-six-sigma.html

7. Six Sigma http://en.wikipedia.org/wiki/Six_Sigma

8. Lean Six Sigma for Software Quality Assurance http://qalibrary.com/qa/lean-six-sigma-for-software-quality-assurance/

9. Bene?ts, obstacles, and future of six sigma approach http://home.gwu.edu.

2

Six Sigma And Users Satisfaction: A Case Study of Ness Wadia College of Commerce Pune, Academic Community

Mr. Manojkumar Thakur

Librarian, Ness Wadia College of Commerce, 19, Late Prin. V.K. Joag Path, Pune

Mrs. Surekha R. Khare

Asstt. Librarian, Ness Wadia College of Commerce, 19, Late Prin. V.K. Joag Path

Mrs. Urmila L. Jagtap

Librarian, Army Institute of Technology, Dighi Hills, Alandi Road, Pune

ABSTRACT

The soul objective of any library, make possible efforts to achieve the goals and objectives of the parent organization by catering need of the users. A periodical review and evaluation of collection and services of the library is highly essential to provide effective and efficient library services. It is crucial to design and develop library services which will assured maximum users satisfaction. The concept of six sigma is to eliminate defects and can be applied in library field to maximize the users satisfaction by eliminating their complaints and problems. The aim of this paper is study the six sigma application in the library as a tool ,to provide efficient services to the clientele of Ness Wadia College of Commerce, Pune. For collection of data a questionnaire based survey method will be adopted. It can be conclude that applying six sigma technique , the library staff will come to know its lacking areas and will be helpful for improvement in better services.

Key Words:- Six Sigma, User Satisfaction, Library Services

INTRODUCTION

Library is a place where information is acquired, stored, classified, and disseminate as and when the user needs. To satisfy the users need, the library should have quality management in libraries. So we have define the actual needs of the library users by focusing on their demands, measure, and control over it.

The concept of six sigma is to eliminate defects. The main aim of application of six sigma in the library is that if you can measure the defects in a process, you can systematically find out ways to eliminate the defect, to approach a quality level of zero defects. Six sigma started in the 1980's at Motorola, then organizations such as GE, Allied Signal, and Seagate worked with the initiative during the 1990s and made it the most successful business initiative of the era.

COLLEGE PROFILE

The Ness Wadia College of Commerce was established on 15th July 1969.

Courses Offered and annual intake of Students

Sr. no.	*Particulars*	*Courses*	*Intake*
1	undergraduates	xi and xii	1200
2	degree courses	b.com, bba, bbm(ib), bca	3120
3	post graduate courses	m.com i and ii	240
4	post graduate diplomas	pgdtl, pgdib, pg diploma in banking and finance	360
		Total	**4920**

There are 9 departments and 71 faculty members and our college is recognized as Research Center for Ph.D.

LIBRARY

A college having well equipped library. Our goal throughout has been to strive for excellence and each day we take a step forward in time and near to our goal that is to provide reading material to our faculty and student, ultimately resulting to fulfill our institute goal that is to impart Commerce and Business Education to the young generation of India. Library is fully automated.

Library has obtained SOUL LIBRARY SOFTWARE Developed by UGC INFLIBNET CENTRE, Ahmedabad.

Library's Stock of Reading Material

Sr. No.	*Particulars*	*Total*
1	Books	48355
2	Journals	111
3	Newspapers	18
4	Bound Volumes	1200
5	Thesis/Dissertation/Project Reports	740
6	Audio-visual Material	277

OBJECTIVES

- To implement the six sigma application in the library as a tool, to provide efficient services to the clientele.
- To evaluate the existing library services.
- To find out the users requirement.
- To try overcome the problems and find out proper solutions to achieve the goal.

RESEARCH METHODOLOGY

For collecting necessary data a questionnaire based survey method was adopted. Keeping in view the objectives in mind a questionnaire is prepared with multiple choice to collect data from the Third year B.Com student and faculty members of Ness Wadia College of Commerce. 225 questionnaires have been distributed to the users and 195 questionnaires were returned by the respondents with response being 86.66% and interpreted for the outcome and presented in the following table.

Table 1. Size of the Sample

Sr. No.	*Respondent*	*Sample*	*%*
1.	Student	160	82.05
2.	Faculty	35	17.94
	Total	195	99.99%

METHODOLOGIES OF SIX SIGMA

There are two types of methodologies in six sigma

DMAIC - define, measure, analyze, improve and control.

DMADV- Define, measure, analyze, design and verify, which is used to create new product designs or process designs.

In this study we have applied DMAIC method. This method is insisting to have continuous assessment, improvement, and guide to bring excellent services to the library users to satisfy them at the maximum.

1. Define – Define the demands of the users and
2. Measure – Measure it.
3. Analyze – Analyze the same
4. Improve – Improve the quality to satisfy the users
5. Control – Make in control

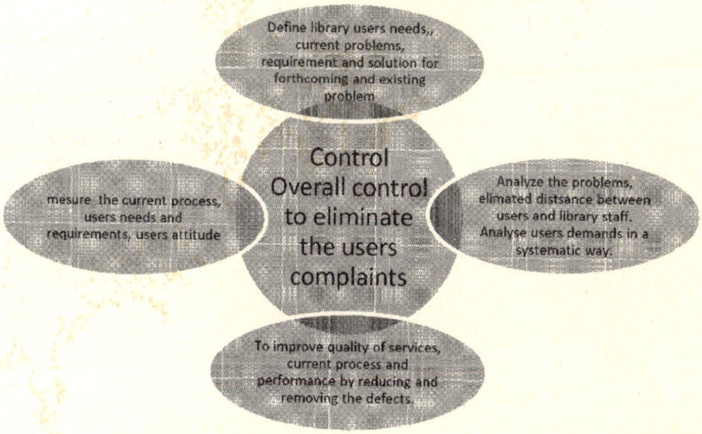

BASIC PROCEDURE OF DMAIC IS

- The users requirements are captured.
- The requirements are analyzed and give priority to the requirements.
- To take action according to requirements.
- A control plan is established.

STEPS IN SIX SIGMA

1. **Define** – In this step we have to find out what is problem, define it clearly and analyze from where it starts. Here we come to know the existing problems and makes us to have our own objectives. Based on users needs and demands we can define and set the objectives and goals to meet their needs.

2. **Measure** – The purpose of this stage is to collect the data and facts related to problems with users. Measurement will be

done based on collection and analysis, to understand the process. In libraries we have to measure the available sources and services, attitude and behavior of the library users and library staff. And lastly set up measureable and achievable targets or goals to cater better services.

3. Analyze – In this stage analyze the origin of the problem and to minimize the distance between the library users and library staff.

4. Improve – This stage makes to improve the library condition from past to present and help us to do better in future. We can improve the procedure and try to find out the new ideas, plans , and ways to do better than the previous to attract the library users. Efficient and systematic approach is must to improve the quality services.

5. Control – This step helps you to review and update the process. It takes overall control of all the steps. Here we have control existing systems and policies to prevent repetition of the problems and eliminate the library users complaints. We have to improve the efficiency of the library staff to satisfy the user's needs.

This methodology analyze process in order to route out sources of unacceptable variations and developed alternatives to eliminate or reduced errors and variations once improvements are implemented controls are put in place to ensure sustained result

Data Analysis

Q.1 : Do you think the present library timing is suitable

Response	*Student*	*%*	*Faculty*	*%*	*Overall*
Y	145	90.62	35	100	92.30
N	12	7.5	00	—	6.15
NR	03	1.87	00	—	1.53
Total	160	99.99	35	100	99.98

Q. 2 : Do you feel the library atmosphere :

Response	*Student*	*%*	*Faculty*	*%*	*Overall*
Pleasant	18	11.25	05	14.28	11.79
Good	98	61.25	19	54.28	60
Poor	43	26.87	09	25.71	26.66
NR	01	0.62	02	5.71	1.53
Total	**160**	**99.99**	**35**	**99.98**	**99.98**

Q.3 : How frequently do you visit the library?

Response	*Student*	*%*	*Faculty*	*%*	*Overall*
Daily	48	30	12	34.28	30.76
Weekly	77	48.12	13	37.14	46.15
Fortnightly	12	7.5	04	11.42	8.20
Monthly	09	5.62	01	2.85	5.12
Any Other	14	8.75	05	14.28	9.74
Total	**160**	**99.99**	**35**	**99.97**	**99.97**

Q.4 : Do you think the present book limit (Two books for one week) for students is sufficient?

Response	*Student*	*%*	*Faculty*	*%*	*Overall*
Y	72	45	20	57.14	47.17
N	88	55	13	37.14	51.79
NR	—	—	02	5.71	1.0
Total	**160**	**100**	**35**	**99.99**	**99.98**

Q. 5 : Do you find library collection updated as per your need?

Response	*Student*	*%*	*Faculty*	*%*	*Overall*
Y	94	58.75	25	71.42	61.02
N	61	38.12	10	28.57	36.41
NR	05	3.12	—	—	2.56
Total	**160**	**99.99**	**35**	**99.99**	**99.99**

Q. 6 : Do you get the books you demand?

Response	*Student*	*%*	*Faculty*	*%*	*Overall*
Y	86	53.75	30	85.71	59.48
N	66	41.12	04	11.42	35.89
NR	08	5	01	2.85	4.61
Total	160	99.87	35	99.98	99.98

Q.7 : Do you find OPAC Facility of the library helping readers to get their book?

Response	*Student*	*%*	*Faculty*	*%*	*Overall*
Y	96	60	24	68.57	61.53
N	43	26.87	00	—	22.05
NR	21	13.12	11	31.42	16.41
Total	160	99.99	35	99.99	99.99

Q. 8 : Do you find the OPAC and Catalogue user Friendly?

Response	*Student*	*%*	*Faculty*	*%*	*Overall*
Y	89	55.62	19	54.28	55.38
N	46	28.75	02	5.71	24.61
NR	25	15.62	14	40	20
Total	160	99.99	35	99.99	99.99

Q. 9 : The main purpose that you use the library is for

Response	*Student*	*%*	*Faculty*	*%*	*Overall*
Study Books	86	53.75	27	77.14	57.94
Check Information	55	34.37	20	57.14	38.46
N/P & Magazines	32	20	10	28.57	21.53
Practical Work	89	55.62	3	8.57	47.17
Internet	06	3.75	3	8.57	4.61
Other	15	9.37	4	11.42	9.74

Q.10 : Please rank the following library services as good, best, excellent and poor?

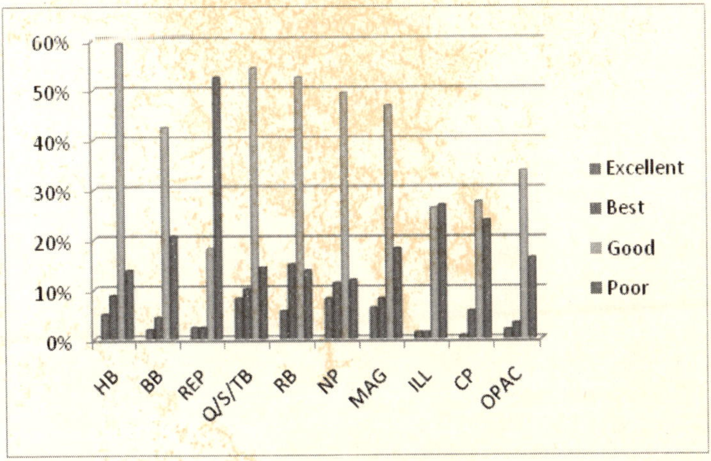

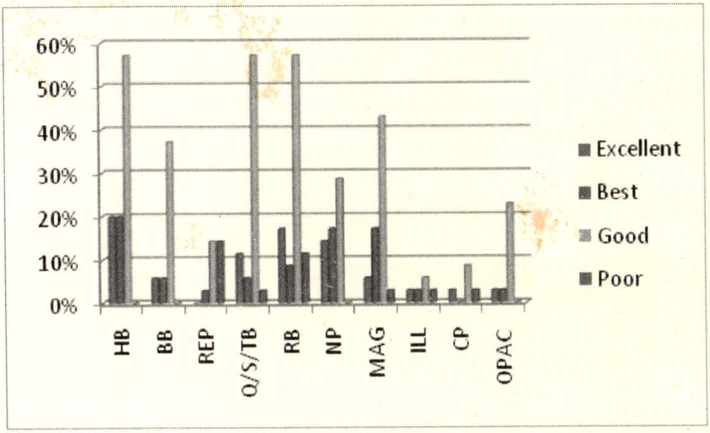

Chart - Student

Q.11 : Do you visit open access reference and periodical section of the library?

Response	*Student*	*%*	*Faculty*	*%*	*Overall*
Y	83	51.87	20	57.14	52.82
N	66	41.25	10	28.57	38.97
NR	11	6.87	05	14.28	8.20
Total	160	99.99	35	99.99	99.99

Q.12 : Do you think library has sufficient space for readers?

Response	*Student*	*%*	*Faculty*	*%*	*Overall*
Y	58	36.25	04	11.42	31.79
N	99	61.87	31	88.57	66.66
NR	03	1.87	—	—	1.53
Total	160	99.99	35	99.99	99.98

Q13 : Have you written on your suggestions in the suggestion Box kept in the library?

Response	*Student*	*%*	*Faculty*	*%*	*Overall*
Y	26	16.25	04	11.42	15.38
N	133	83.12	30	85.71	83.58
NR	01	0.62	01	2.85	1.02
Total	160	99.99	35	99.98	99.98

Q.14 : Do you think library should have separate section for following?

Sections	*Student*	*Faculty*	*Overall %*
Internet Browsing	109	30	71.99
Audio Visual	69	23	47.17
Reading Room	107	33	71.79
Digital Library	76	25	51.79

Q.15 : Do you think library should purchase recreational CD's, VCD's and movies?

Response	*Student*	*%*	*Faculty*	*%*	*Overall*
Y	119	74.37	32	91.42	77.43
N	38	23.75	02	5.71	20.51
NR	03	1.87	01	2.85	2.05
Total	160	99.99	35	99.98	99.99

Q.16 : What do think about the behavior of the library staff?

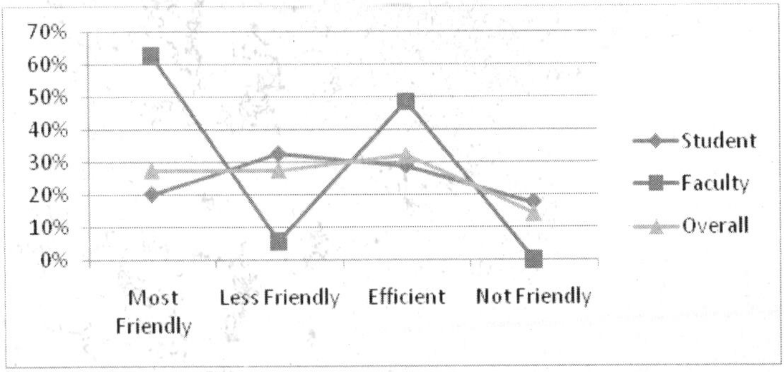

Q. 17 : Do the library staff help you in finding the books and other reading material?

Response	*Student*	*%*	*Faculty*	*%*	*Overall*
Y	128	80	34	97.14	83.07
N	29	18.12	00	00	14.87
NR	03	1.87	01	2.85	2.05
Total	160	99.99	35	99.99	99.99

Q.18 : How would you like to rank our library?

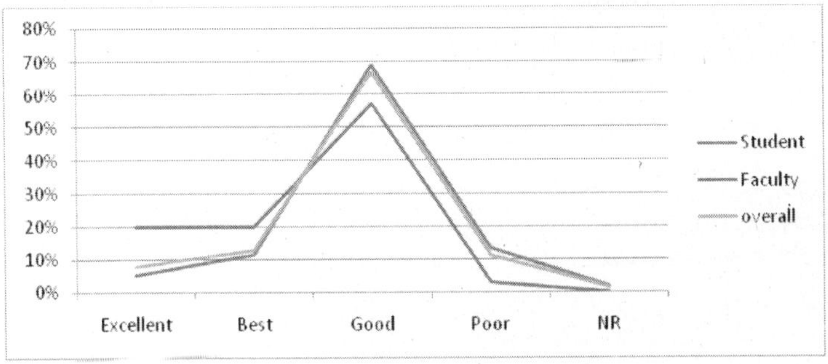

Q.19 : Do you think there should be a grievances committee of students and college authorities?

Response	*Student*	*%*	*Faculty*	*%*	*Overall*
Y	110	68.75	29	82.85	71.28
N	39	24.37	03	8.57	21.53
NR	11	6.87	03	8.57	7.17
Total	160	99.99	35	99.99	99.98

From the above tables and charts we identify the problems of clientele of library and found the following solutions on it.

1. Most of the users found that library has limited space.
2. 61% students and 54% of the staff feel that library atmosphere is good and 11% student and 14% faculty feels pleasant library atmosphere.
3. 30.76% of the users are visiting library daily. Most of the users are visiting library weekly.
4. Most of the students are not satisfied with the present book limit.
5. Overall 61.02% users are satisfied with library collection.
6. 59.48% respondent is getting their required books within time.
7. 61.53% users are aware about OPAC Facility and they found it is helpful to get their books.
8. Maximum students are using library for issue of study book, news papers, magazines and question papers and practical work. Most of the users demand separate section for internet browsing.
9. Content page, Inter library Loan, OPAC and reprography services were ranked poor and 38.97% user were not using Open access periodical and reference sections.
10. Overall 27.69% users are feel library staff is less friendly. Overall 28% users ranked library as poor.

Future Plans for Solutions

1. Library space will be increased and library is planning to

have separate reading room for faculty and reading hall for students.

2. For pleasant atmosphere necessary arrangement of ventilation and lights will be made.
3. Library will organize orientation program for students.
4. Library is planning to issue three books for two weeks to the students for home reading.
5. A register will be maintained at issue counter to record shortage copies.
6. Library staff of circulation section will be train and instructed to improve their performance.
7. Those who are not aware about OPAC facility, a brochure namely "How to Use OPAC" will be displayed and library staff will be instructed to assist them.
8. Library has informed the college authorities to provide sufficient space to have separate section for internet browsing, digital library, audio visual sections.
9. It is observed that many readers are not aware of the library services such as content page, ILL, OPAC, for them user orientation program will be conducted.
10. A training program regarding efficient customer service will be arranged for library staff.

    To provide better services library will conduct periodical review of collection and services, invite suggestions etc.
11. 71.28% users feel that there should be a student grievances committee to solve grievance. The college authorities will be informed to have efficient and effective grievances committee.

CONCLUSION

There is acute problem of library space. Most of the services were not used efficiently because users are not aware of these services. There is a strong need of library orientation and communication skills to be provided to the library staff and users.

REFERENCES

1. Al-Zubi, Ahmed Ali and Basha, Imtiaz.2010. Six Sigma in libraries: A management perspectives. Canadian Journal on Computing in Mathematics, Natural Sciences, Engineering and Medicine 1(3), pp 86-93 Accessed from http://www.ampublisher.com on 3/8/2011

2. Billington, M.G. and Billington, P.J. 2006 Training for Six Sigma. In Sisodiya, Amit Singh(Ed). Six Sigma : Concepts and Cases. (pp62-69). Hyderabad: ICFAI University Press.

3. Bruce, Greg and Launsby, Robert G. 2005. Design for Six Sigma Tata McGraw-Hill, New Delhi

4. Bruce, Greg 2002. Six Sigma for Managers. Tata McGraw-Hill, New Delhi

5. Chakrabarty, Ayon and Chuan, Tan Kay.The Extent of Six Sixma Methodologies usage in services.Accessed from http://www.iamot.org on 3/8/2011

6. Kaushik, Chitra etc.2007. Six Sigma application for library services. DESIDOC Bulletin of Information Technology, 27(5) pp 35-39 Accessed from http://www. Publications.drdo.gov.in on 3/8/2011

7. McCarty, Tom etc. 2010 The Six sigma Black Belt Handbook. Tata McGraw-Hill, New Delhi

8. Sisodiya, Amit Singh 2006. Six Sigms : Concepts and Cases.

3

Comparative Study of ISO and Six Sigma

Vrushali Dandawate
Librarian, AISSMS COE, Pune
Ajay Khatri
Librarian, SRC Ayurved Medical College, Chikhli
Pradip Umdale
Information Specialist, GE, Banglore

ABSTARCT

Quality management has become increasingly present in the life of organizations. Their survival is mainly linked to the quality of their activities. The way in which each organization focuses on quality issues may vary according to the sectors and the environment where it carries out its activities and of course, the organization's own strategies. There are various ways of focusing on quality and one of the options is to approach the quality management system using the standard ISO 9001and Six Sigma approach. This paper try to compare this two approach of quality management.

Keywords: Quality management, Six Sigma, ISO Certification, Customer Satisfaction

INTRODUCTION OF ISO

The ISO approach towards quality management concentrates on standardization of the activities of production. The eight quality principles of ISO 9000, along with its twenty-four requirements outline business processes. The emphasis here is on the control of events in each aspect of doing business by documenting evidence and reports. The eight principles of ISO 9000 include prioritizing customer data, purchasing and quality systems, among other critical aspects. ISO 9000 recognizes each process, whose end goals are the same, as an independent entity. Documented quality requirements typically decide, based on set rules, whether or not a particular process adhered to that standard. Since its initial publication in 1987, the number of implementations of ISO 9000 quality systems has increased year after year in the business context and it has led to a growing number of business information services being managed using these standards. The first review of this series of standards was carried out in 1994, and the second review and the publication of the edition in force took place in 2000. The ISO 9000 series includes several standards but, at present, the only one that is certifiable is the ISO 9001. An ISO 9001 certification should assure a company's customers that minimum acceptable systems, processes and procedures are in place to ensure product and service quality can be met. ISO 9001 provides the basis for documenting the knowledge of your processes and thus serves as a fundamental training mechanism. As continual improvement is undertaken the new or revised approach is standardized through revision of your procedures and instructions. The ISO 9001 standard is also slowly being adopted in public institutions, where still there are few information services and libraries that have opted to manage their quality system with ISO 9001:2000.

INTRODUCTION OF SIX SIXMA

Six Sigma is a business management strategy originally developed by Motorola, USA in 1986. As of 2010[update], it is widely used in many sectors of industry, although its use is not without controversy. Six Sigma seeks to improve the quality of process outputs by identifying and removing the causes of defects and minimizing variability in manufacturing and business processes. It uses a set of quality management methods, including statistical methods, and creates a special infrastructure of people within the organization ("Black Belts", "Green Belts", etc.) who are experts in these methods. Each Six Sigma project carried out within an organization follows a defined sequence of steps and has quantified financial targets (cost reduction and/or profit increase.

The term *Six Sigma* originated from terminology associated with manufacturing, specifically terms associated with statistical modeling of manufacturing processes. The maturity of a manufacturing process can be described by a sigma rating indicating its yield, or the percentage of defect-free products it creates. A six sigma process is one in which 99.99966% of the products manufactured are statistically expected to be free of defects (3.4 defects per million). Motorola set a goal of "six sigma" for all of its manufacturing operations, and this goal became a byword for the management and engineering practices used to achieve.Six Sigma projects follow two project methodologies inspired by Deming's Plan-Do-Check-Act Cycle. These methodologies, composed of five phases each, bear the acronyms DMAIC and DMADV. DMAIC is used for projects aimed at improving an existing business process DMAIC is pronounced as "duh-may-ick".DMADV is used for projects aimed at creating new product or process designs.DMADV is pronounced as "duh-mad-vee".

CERTIFICATION

Although no official accrediting agency exists in the United States, Six Sigma certification for both Green and Black Belts is offered by several independent providers. Many organizations also offer certification programs to their employees. Corporations, such as early Six Sigma pioneers General Electric and Motorola developed certification programs as part of their Six Sigma implementation.

COMPARISON OF ISO WITH SIX SIGMA

ISO 9001 and Six Sigma serve two different purposes. ISO 9001 is a quality management system, while Six Sigma is a strategy and methodology for business performance improvement. ISO 9001, with guidelines for problem solving and decision making, requires a continual improvement process in place but does not indicate what the process should look like. Six Sigma can provide the needed improvement process. However, it does not provide a template for evaluating an organization's overall quality management efforts whereas ISO9001 does.

On the other hand, ISO 9001 simply suggests that your business should take a factual Approach to Decision Making. This means making informed decisions and ensuring data and information are sufficiently accurate and reliable and accessible to those who need it. ISO 9001 wants you to use the facts but to also balance it with experience and intuition.

Major theme of ISO 9001 is Continual Improvement. Unlike Six Sigma, ISO 9001 puts innovation squarely on the roadmap for organizational success. It's all about numbers and not about customers

ISO 9001 makes it abundantly clear throughout the standard that Customer Focus is a key element to business success.

Six Sigma = cost cutting. while ISO 9001 reminds us that in addition to cutting costs, we also have to focus on Mutually Beneficial Supplier Relationships, Leadership, Involvement of People and more.

Six Sigma = micromanaging, while ISO 9001 is anything but micromanaging if it is well-implemented by an experienced consultant. The standard only required six documented procedures. A smooth-running ISO 9001 certified company is one that operates on its own positive, organic momentum.

Criteria	ISO 9000	Six Sigma
Developed By	ISO	Motorola
Focus	Product	Product and Process
Cerification	External Agency	Internal Control
Function	Define Methodology	Defined Values
Applicability	All types of Industries	All Industries
Approch	Quality assurance Approach	DMAC & DMAV approach
Technique used	Qualitative Techniques	Statistical Techniques
Working	Review entire quality management system	Reviews only specific project process
Limitation	Lacking in guidance to improve quality	Lack of Certified Authority

(Difference between ISO 9000 and Six Sigma)

COMBINING SIX SIGMA WITH ISO

Six Sigma provides a methodology for delivering certain quality objectives set by ISO 9001 such as: prevention of defects at all stages from design through servicing Statistical techniques required for establishing, controlling and verifying process capability and product characterization Investigation of the cause of defects relating to product, process and the quality system continual improvement of the quality of products and services. Six Sigma supports ISO and helps an organization satisfying the ISO requirements.

ISO is an excellent vehicle for documenting and maintaining the process management system involving Six Sigma. Extensive training is required by both systems for successful deployment.

CONCLUSION

Six Sigma and ISO are is generally used in manufacturing sectors to minimize the wastages and to assure the quality in such a way the same can be implemented in libraries to develop the process and improve the standard of the library to satisfy the users. Six Sigma and ISO helps to improve the standard of the library and helps to improve the skills and ability of the library employees. It insists on continues improvement and development of the library as well as library staff members. The ultimate goal of the library is to satisfy its users. This can be achievable by the Six Sigma as well as ISO. It helps library employees to have a better management to evaluate the services to library users.

REFERENCES

1. http://www.sriregistrar.com
2. http://ezinearticles.com/
3. "The Inventors of Six Sigma". Retrieved August 29, 2011.
4. SIX SIGMA: SPC and TQM in Manufacturing and Services. Gower Publishing, Ltd.. p. 6.
5. Antony, Jiju. "Pros and cons of Six Sigma: an academic perspective" .
6. http://EzineArticles.com
7. De Feo, J.A. and W. Barnard, 2005. Juran Institute's Six Sigma Breakthrough and Beyond-Quality Performance Breakthrough Methods. Tata McGraw-Hill Publishing Company Limited.
8. Hamza, S.E.A., 2008. Design process improvement through the DMAIC Six Sigma approach: A case study from the Middle East. Int. J. Six Sigma Competit. Advant., 4:35-47.
9. Kim, D.S., 2006. A study on Introducing Six sigma theory in the Library for service Competitiveness enhancement. IFLA, Proceeding of the World Library and Information Congress, 72nd IFLA General Conference and Council, Aug. 20-24, Seoul, Korea, pp:1-16. http://ifla.queenslibrary.org/IV/ifla72/pape rs/146-Kim-en.pdf
10. http://www.asq.org/learn-about-quality/project-planning-tools/overview/pdsa-cycle.html

4

Six Sigma In Libraries

Dr. (Mrs.) Khaparde V. S.
Asso. Prof. & HOD, Dept. of LIS, Dr. BAMU, Aurangabad

Mr. Chopkar H. D.
Research Student Dept. of LIS, Dr. BAMU, Aurangabad

ABSTRACT

Six Sigma is now increasingly being applied to wide range of process ranging from manufacturing to services and variegated transactional process. A fundamental objective of six sigma is to achieve user satisfaction .Doing this right and keeping them consistent are the ideas behind six sigma. The purpose of any library is to be pleased to all user needs. Users are the back bone of library and they are best judges to evaluate the service and quality of the library. But in general, it is difficult to satisfy completely and totally of every user needs. To evaluate "users satisfaction" and to develop the quality of the library, it is mandatory to bring a new innovation. To develop the library and to provide maximum users satisfaction, it is necessary to implement six sigma in libraries.

Keywords : Six Sigma, Library Services, User Satisfaction, Management.

INTRODUCTION

The eventual goal of any library is users satisfaction. Six sigma help us to do continues appraisal and improve the quality of the library to satisfy the library users in an effective and better manner. Six Sigma will improve the quality of the library, maximizing the users satisfaction and promote better performance. This paper is insisting to implement six sigma in library field. The principals of this study is to seek for applications of six sigma as a results for well - organized alertness administration. In addition it aims to launch information infrastructure and secure service in the competitive world to improve user satisfaction. The term six sigma process comes from the notion that if one has six standard deviations between the mean of a process and the nearest specification limit, there will be practically no items that fail to meet the specification.

DEFINITION

Six Sigma is a methodology and set of tools used to improve quality to than 3.4 defects per million or better. Six Sigma is uniquely driven by close understanding of customer needs, disciplined use of facts, data, and statistical analysis and diligent attention to managing improving and reinventing. Six Sigma stands for six Standard Deviations (Sigma is Greek letter used to represent standard deviation in statistics) from mean. It is statistically based methodology for improving product quality to meet the uses needs

BENEFITS OF SIX SIGMA

Following benefits of Six Sigma

1. Six Sigma helps to understand and manage customer requirement
2. Line up the key business process to achieve the needed requirements
3. Exploit accuracy in data analysis to minimize defects in the process
4. Bring fast development and continue improvement to business process
5. Minimizing the effort and maximizing the profit

6. Helps to work smart rather than hard
7. Bringing the efficiency among employers.

SIX STEPS TO SIX SIGMA

Step 1: Identify the product we create or the service you provide.

Step 2: Identify the customers for your product or service and determine what they consider important.

Step 3: Identify your needs (to provide product / service so that it satisfies the customer)

Step 4: Define the process for doing the work.

Step 5: Mistake-proof the process and eliminate wasted effort.

Step 6: Ensure continuous improvement by measuring ,analyzing and controlling the improved process.

KEY CONCEPTS OF SIX SIGMA

In general Six Sigma has few concepts such as critical to Quality, Defects, Process Capability and Stable Operation.

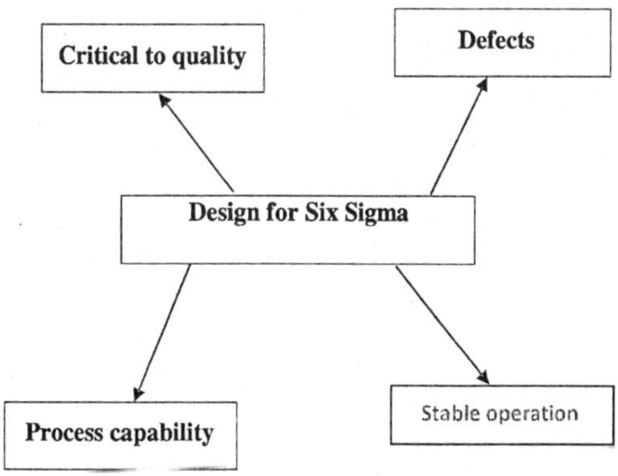

Fig. 1. Key Concepts of Six Sigma

1. Critical to quality : This is one of the concepts of six sigma which insists to have attachment with users. In general if we have close relationship and contact with users, we may easily come to know their needs, demands and complaints. The base for the quality is to know the important and signification need of the users.

2. **Defects** : This process helps us to overcome the failures at the same it will help to minimize the defects. When eliminate the defects simultaneously can reach the point of what users wants.

3. **Process capability** : This step helps to analyze to know the capability and capacity to process the delivery. through this course we can analyze and improve the procedure to deliver our goods to customers.

4. **Stable operation** : Every action has its own reaction. Likewise if we follow the above methods, we can develop the consistency, can predict, can process and can improve the exactly customer sees and feels.

SERVICE QUALITY EVALUATION

Service quality evaluation of the library is analysis of service efficacy. Efficacy of the service quality evaluation is not restricted to the fact that service is simply provided to the user. It also focuses on the degree of utilization by users demand for information and their satisfaction in terms of quality and quantity. If quality evaluation is the number of inquiries and answers recorded in the resource center of the library then service quality and how many answers actually helped the users. In fact, assessing the service quality is the most difficult phase of the evaluation. Unlike tangible commodities that can be evaluated objectively, service cannot be easily defined and measured due to its distinctive features. Therefore, service quality is a subjective quality rather than an objective one. It is defined as perceived service quality by user. Regarding evaluating the service quality of the library

CONCLUSIONS

Libraries in the process of applying six sigma must perceive the factor that satisfies users as an ideal quality and try to find key factors that affect quality from users point of view. Moreover, libraries are made to collect objective and reliable data and employ methods of statistic analysis in order to gather data and information within the organization and use them for decision – making. As a characteristic of library service, however, there are generally distributed factors which are impossible to control or hard to quantify. Therefore, it is necessary to consider the respect that it is difficult to define problems of current service and users complaints.

REFERENCES

- Al-Zubi, Ahmad Ali;Basha Imtiaz (2010) Six Sigma in libraries: A management perspective. *Canadian journal on computing in mathematics, natural science, engineering and medicine*, 1(3), 86-93
- Coronado, R; Antony, J. (2002) Critical success factors for the implementation of Six Sigma project in organization. The TQM Management, 14(2), 92-99.
- Kaushik, Chitra; Shokeen Ashu; Kaushik Prabhakar (2007) Six Sigma application for library services. DESIDOC Bulletin of information technology, 27(5)35-39.
- Kumar, P. (2002) Six Sigma in manufacturing. Production Journal, 43(2), 196-202.
- Prabhushankar G.V; Devadasan, S.R; Shalij, P.R (2008) Six Sigma in Indian Automotive Components Sector: A Survey. The ICFAI University Journal of Operation Management, 7(3), 18.
- Sambhe, Rajeshkumar.U. Dalu, Rajendra S (2011) Evaluating Six Sigma implantation in Medium Scale Indian Automotive Enterprises. International Journal of Engineering and Technology, 3(3), 1790-1796.
- Wesel, G.; Burcher, P (2008) Six Sigma for small and medium – sized enterprises. TQM Magzine, 16(4)264-272.

5

A Comprehensive Approach to Library Improvement Through Six Sigma

Dr. RK Kishore Patnala (PhD)
I/c Librarian ISB&M School of Technology Nande village, Pune-42

ABSTRACT

In order for a library to reach its real prospective when it comes to quality improvement through six sigma. A comprehensive approach must be taken in its efforts by incorporating enrichment, process improvement, leadership commitment, strategic operation, integrated infrastructure, disciplined framework, user satisfaction and staff development. Libraries may not only reach their desired results faster and easily but able to maintain integrity and reliability of the change that are made.

Keywords : six sigma, library, comprehensive approach

INTRODUCTION

Assessment of user satisfaction in library services, we need reasonable and professional assessment tools for user satisfaction and performance measurement. In this paper get started to draw and implement scientific and systematic improvement plans for service area that failed to meet its goal or caused users complaints.

Six sigma means " a systematic innovative activity to statistical measure and analyze cause of defects that happen in all parts of management, and then remove those causes."

According to six sigma, defects include all causes that disrupt development or service. It is methodology to define a problem from the viewpoint of managers or users as a defect and determine its causes in order to solve it. As a theory it was originally used in manufacturing. Now a day's six sigma applied to service fields also. In this paper find out the user complaint factors and reduce them. This paper helps to identify the application plans of six sigma and its impact in the library field.

SIX SIGMA FOR THE SERVICE IMPROVEMENT

Six Sigma management is defined as a systemic and innovative activity that assesses the causes for the defects and an error occurred in every sector of the management based on the statistical measure, analyzes the causes and ultimately eliminates them.

Definition of the defects in six sigma includes all factors that hold back process or service. Unlike the conventional improvement methodology which focuses on minimizing defects in the manufacturing venue or on the problems solving in the specific field, the six sigma defines defect as a problem arising in a sectors of the company that is perceived problematic by the management or by the user. So six sigma is a methodology that thoroughly pinpoints the causes of such defects and eliminates them fundamentally.

Primarily in 1930-50's focused on the improving the quality of manufacturing process that knows as a Quality Control (QC) after that in 1960's Total Quality Control focused on small group activity, comprehensive problem solving etc, later on 1980's

Total Quality Management ISO 9000 for improvement the quality approval and quality management and 1990 onwards Six Sigma for process innovation, quality improvement of the direct sector. The major difference of the Six Sigma from the quality improvement movements (quality control, Total quality Control and Total Quality Management) is elimination of the possibility of defects. Eliminating the defects in beginning that is literary meaning of the quality improvement. In six sigma all the work or processes are assess and calculate Sigma Quality. Finally reach the six sigma level.

The term sigma is a sign indicates values that measure dispersion in statistics and it originates from the small letter sigma in the Greek language. Sigma as a target value to be achieved by corporate management. According to the six sigma is a technique in which superior goal of the minimum defect or error ratio is set to the level of 3.4/1,000,000 and the company strives to achieve such high standard. Further user demands are identified transformed into the task to be solved and optimal specification is determined based on the interrelation among each task (Defeo, 1999) it is a management innovation technique that applies scientific statistical techniques in all processes for the user satisfaction, achieves high product quality and contributes to the enhancement of the management performance.

The Six Sigma is conducted with a project-centered method that is fundamentally based on the 'Black belt', the problem-solver. This 'problem-solving' phase is called DMAIC (Figure 1). First projects are defined from the perspective of customers or regarding process (Define). Second based on the defined projects, the current level of the product quality is measured into sigma level (Measure). Third causes of the problems are detected through the analysis so as to improve the sigma level (Analyze). Fourth efforts are made to improve the situation by working with the causes of the problems (Improve). Finally the optimal condition generated by the above mentioned phases are controlled, maintained and monitored (Control).

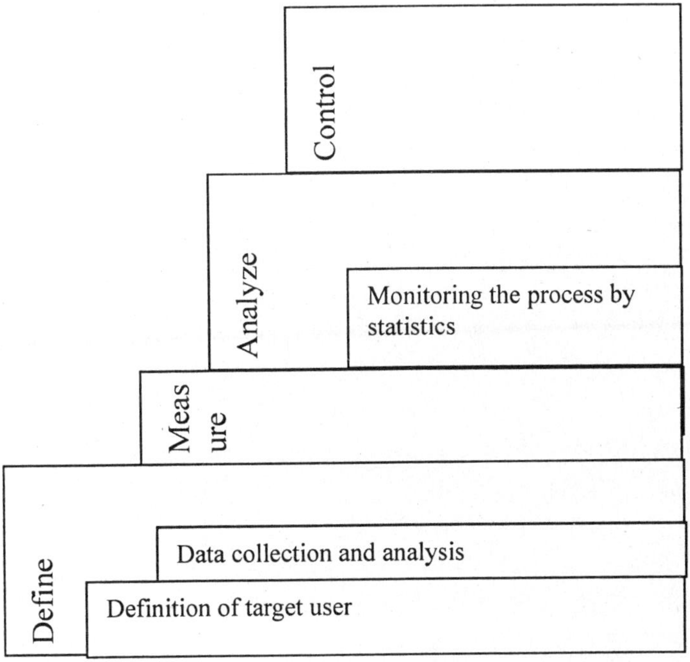

Fig. 1. DMAIC

PROSPECT OF THE SIX SIGMA APPLICATION IN LIBRARY

If the library service is evaluated from the user's perspective through quality evaluation tools such as LibQUAL+, how will the follow-up process improve service, the organization, the attitude of the librarian and the process which are below the user expectation? If the improvement plans based on such evaluation are not successful in the following year, the next evaluation will produce the same results. Therefore, it should be examined how the Six Sigma theory as a follow-up of the evaluation can be applied more scientifically and systematically to the library process.

Investment on the collection of books and improvement of the communication with the user include elements that could be or could not be defined as a process. It is possible to pinpoint the cause of the discrepancy between the plan and the actual result and the process to be improved the most in terms of the general quality improvement and user satisfaction. Utilize process analysis method and Six Sigma statistical method for the successful Six Sigma management of the library. The Six Sigma management originally used for the manufacturing industry must be modified and characterized as the process apt for the service industry. The process is an assembly of activities which convert input such as information and human resources into output such as product and service. Process analysis is to identify a key process by concentrating on the satisfaction of the user needs.

PROCESS CONTROL

1. Define
2. Measure
3. Analysis
4. Improve
5. Control

DPU = total defects / total products per unit

Defects per unit (DPU) are an important parameter for library improvement a company in Texas, USA made a survey on the customer satisfaction. In that questionnaire item, 'very dissatisfied' was counted as 0 point and 'very satisfied' as 9 point. Total 10 tiers from 0 to 9 points were calculated to examine the customer satisfaction. In the questionnaire filled out by the customer, a customer with the total point below 5 was considered as having dissatisfaction with the company. Such case was assessed as a defect. DPU was calculated from the number of 'defect customers' and it was converted back to the sigma level. As a result of the customer satisfaction survey, 7 customers out of 286 turned out to have below 5 point total, hence dissatisfied with the company in that survey.

Accordingly, DPU = 7/286 = 0.02448 and corresponding ratio thereof is $e^{-0.002448}$ = 0.9758. The sigma level was calculated as follows.

$$Zs = \Phi{-}1(0.9758) + 1.5 = 1.97 + 1.5 = 3.47$$

Calculation of the sigma level with the categorical type data of the survey requires objective standard that determines defects in the particular organization.

CONCLUSIONS

Six Sigma is a management approach with total quality control that uses statistic measure called 'sigma' to evaluate all the quality levels quantitatively under the strong leadership of Librarian, provides efficient quality control environment including problem-solving process and professional training, and promotes quality improvement and user satisfaction. Focused on the user perspective, the Six Sigma detects problem of process and proposes the solution in which the project is solved through the statistically-liable procedures. In this study the possibility of such a solution is examined in order to apply it as a follow-up improvement task after the library evaluation. Under the user survey through the questionnaire analysis and assess the library environment. CTQ of the user select suitable plans for library. DMAIC steps performed in accordance with the six sigma strategy. CTQ satisfies user demands; moreover applications of statistical technique control the defects and improve the quality and attention to the daily works in the library.

Library quality and quality control is essential and also the librarian will-power, leadership skills and positive thinking on the six sigma will definitely improve the library. Implement those six sigma application in daily works, that effort can improve library value and enhancement of the user satisfaction. Six Sigma theories is used in order to review various aspects of library management, conduct evaluation and find a service process necessary for improvement to raise user satisfaction.

REFERENCE

- Defeo, J.A. (1999). "Six Sigma: Road Map for Survival." H.B.R. Focus Vol.76.
- Harry, M.J. Talk about six sigma. Green Belt Training Report. General Electric Company, India, 2001.

- Henderson, K.M. & Evans, J.R. Successful implementation of six sigma. Benchmarking.Int. J. Benchmarking, 2002, 7(4), 260-82.
- Kim, Dong Suk(2006). A study on the service quality evaluation of University Library applying the LibQUAL+.
- Maleyeff, J. & Krayenvenger, D.E. Goal setting with six sigma mean shift determination. Air Engg. Aero. Tech., 2004, 76(2), 577-83.
- O'Neill, M. & Duvall, C. A six sigma quality approach to workplace evaluation. J. Facil. Manag., 2004, 3(2), 240-53.
- Suk-Kim Dong, a study on introducing six-sigma theory in the library for service competitiveness enhancement.

6

Six Sigma Applications in LIS Field

Shrinivas Athalye
Librarian, Swami Vivekanand Night College, Dombivli

ABSTRACT

Sigma is a statistical concept which used for measurement. There are six levels of measurement assumed in production management, which are known as Six Sigma. With the application of the six sigma, the defects in production and processing are reduced and the satisfaction of the customer is increased. Now in today's Information Technology era, the reader is known as customer and the librarian is as information manager. If the library were a production house, the six sigma is applicable to it also. So that library services can be produced more efficiently to the best satisfaction of the reader. In this research paper, meaning and application of six sigma to library is explained and the experiment of six sigma application carried out in a academic library at Dombivli is also explained.

Keywords : Sigma level, Six sigma, Key players, Sigma application

INTRODUCTION

"Whenever you see a successful business, someone once

made a courageous decision" — Peter Drucker (1919-2005)

Every business or industry runs on the wheels of decisions and systems. Decisions include policy or vision of the business and systems include the procedure or process and the management. Management is one of the most important factors on which the whole business is dependent. That's why, it is also more important to measure or evaluate the management system.

Methods

Six sigma project follows the DMAIC project methodology which means...

Define the problem, the voice of customer and the project goals.

Measure key aspect of the current process and collect relevant data.

Analyze the data to investigate and verify cause and effect relationship. Determine what relationships are and attempt to ensure that all factors have been considered. Seek out root cause of the defect under investigation.

Improve the current process based upon data analysis using techniques such as design of experiment, mistake proofing. Set up pilot runs to establish process capability.

Control the future state process to ensure that any deviations from target are corrected before they result in defects.

LEVELS OF SIGMA PERFORMANCE

In business, the greater the number of defects that occur, the greater the cost of correcting them as well as the risk of losing the customers. A seemingly low percentage of defects can mean a lot of unhappy customers. If a company processed 2,50,000 credit card bills a month and operated at 99.38% accuracy at 4 sigma level. See table no.1. It would have about 1,550 unhappy customers every month.

The goal of six sigma is to help people and processes aim

high in aspiring to deliver defect-free products and services. Six sigma recognizes that there is always some potential for defects, even in the best-run processes or best-built product. But at 99.99966 percent performance, six sigma sets a performance target where defects in many processes and products almost nonexistent.

KEY PLAYERS

Six sigma cannot be managed on the sidelines, it is a full contact sport that sets new rules and aims for much higher scores. Basically there are 5 key players mentioned as under.

1. **Executive Leaders** : These are the persons who have to commit to six sigma and to promote it throughout the origination.

2. **Champions** : Champions fight for the cause of black belts and remove barriers.

3. **Master Black Belts** : These have to serve as trainer, mentor and guide.

4. **Black Belts** : Black Belts have to work full time on projects.

5. **Green Belts** : Green Belts have to assist black belts part time.

SIX SIGMA IN THE FIELD OF LIBRARIES

In today's information technology era, libraries are known as information industries and librarians are information manager. So, if the libraries are industries, then all rules applied to industries are applicable to libraries also. Libraries have also, to manage all its services within time limit and accurate. Libraries afford six sigma levels for the following levels

1. Basically six sigma is not only for improvement in the skill or the quantity of the services, but for deleting defects in the present services also. With its application, defects can be found and moved out and libraries can follow the five laws of library science told by S. R. Ranganathan.
2. Reader is the customer of the library. And to fulfill the

customer's demand, is the motto of the six sigma. So libraries can make satisfied to its customers by adopting the six sigma.

3. Six sigma can improve the number of satisfied customers.
4. Black belts and Green belts are the hands of the body of the libraries. With the defect removing system, their moral can be raised and they can do their job in a better way.
5. In this system, libraries can pay attention at not only perfection in services but at knowledge in all kinds of media also.
6. While going for computerization, the six sigma can find out the delay, slow working and defects in the system.

APPLICATION OF SIX SIGMA IN LIBRARIES

Here, I want to share my experience with a College Library at Dombivli, where computerization was going on, but data entry work was unsatisfactory. All equipments were in good condition, experienced staff was appointed, power failure problem was overruled by the inverter system. This was the situation before the work. See table No.2.

Situation before the work

Table 2 : Situation before the work

Sr. No.	*Particulars*	*Details*
1	Data Entry Target	The library had 12,000 books for data entry.
2	Entry Words	48 words per entry
3	Duration	The work tobe completed within 30 working days
4	Manpower	One data entry operator with the speed of 4o words per minute.
5	Working Hours	8 hours in a day

Source: Field observation

Situation during the work

But the speed and accuracy was not more than 2 levels of

six sigma. The accuracy and peed was 75% out of the work. All were still satisfied, but not the librarian. He found out the solution and made some changes. This was the situation during the work. First of all, he added extra manpower, changed the working hours, replaced the easy chairs with the wooden chairs and lightened the Agarbattis as room fresheners. These things are seems to be very little, but brought up a tremendous change.

Situation after the work

Now the library has reached to the sixth level. This was the situation after the work. See table No.3

Table .3 : Situation after the work

Sr. No.	*Particulars*	*Before*	*After*
1	Syatem used	Ordinary	Six sigma
2	Data entry target	12,000	12,000
3	Duration	30 working days , 8 hours per day	30 working days, 4 hours per day.
4	Manpower	One operator	Two operators
5	Speed	40 wpm	30 wpm
6	Findings	400 entries in a days	600 entries in a day
7	Defects	100 entries	0 entries
8	Result	Work done in 30 days with 75% accuracy	Work done in 20 days with 100% accuracy
9	Sigma level	2	6

Source. Field observation

CONCLUSION

Sigma is used for measurement. It measures a level of accuracy of product, process or service. It is a tool to manage a business. As library is a service house, it is also measurable. With the help of six sigma, a library can improve its services, remove the defects and make its readers more satisfied. The only thing is that one must have courage to implement six sigma with full strength for prestigious improvement in all aspects in future.

REFERENCES

1. Bhote, Keki R. (2007), The power of ultimate sig sigma,Mumbai: jaico,pp.352
2. Brue,Greg (2002), Six sigma for managers, New, Delhi: Tata McGraw-Hill, pp.190
3. Pande, Pete and Holpp, Larry (2002), What is six sigma?, new Delhi: Tata McGraw-Hill, pp88
4. Stamatis, D.H. (2004), Six sigma fundamentals: A complete guide to the systems, methods and tools, New York: Productivity Press, pp.100
5. http://en.wikipedia.org/wiki/Six_Sigma. Retrieved on August 03, 2011
6. http://www.motorola.com/motorolauniversity. Retrieved on August 03, 2011

7

Six Sigma: Modern Management Technique

Mr. Chandanvandan Atul

Librarian, Vidya Pratishthan's Polytechnic College, Indapur

ABSTRACT

Management techniques and principles are developed and formalized to help improve personal or organizational performance, for various forms of human endeavor, in a systematic, efficient, and consistent manner. Today, the library is under pressure to become more efficient while delivering even better experiences for library users. Faced with these challenges, libraries have to modernize nearly every aspect of their operations. Six Sigma can be both an improvement methodology and a corporate strategy. In the latter, the Six Sigma concept is not only applied to individual projects, but to the whole organization, to each area and function Six Sigma as a corporate strategy can lead to real breakthrough improvement.

Key Words : Management, Six Sigma, Six Sigma Belts

INTRODUCTION

In library and information centers the foremost objective is to satisfy the need of its users. Six Sigma is a business management strategy is to improve the quality of process outputs by identifying and removing the causes of defects and minimizing variability in manufacturing and business processes. The intention of the paper is to apply of Six Sigma as a tool for efficient service provider to library users. Six Sigma will improve the quality of the library, maximizing the users' satisfaction and efficient library management

SIX SIGMA

The Six Sigma process improvement originated in 1986 from Motorola's drive towards reducing defects by minimizing variation in processes through metrics measurement. Sigma Sigma , a Greek alphabet, is used in mathematics and statistics to define standard deviation. Six Sigma means "a systematic innovative activity to statistically measure and analyze causes of defects that happen in all parts of management, and then remove those causes." According to Six Sigma, defects include all causes that interrupt process or service. It is a methodology to define a problem from the viewpoint of managers or users as a defect and ascertain its causes in order to solve it.

METHODOLOGIES OF SIX SIGMA

There are two types of methodologies in Six Sigma –

1. DMAIC
2. DMADV

DMAIC stands for Define, Measure, Analyze, Improve and Control. DMAIC, which is used to improve an existing business process DMADV stands for Define, Measure, Analyze, Design and Verify, which is used to create new product designs or process designsBoth are insisting to have Continuous assessment, improvement, and guide to bring excellent services to library users to satisfy them at the maximum

DMAIC, methodology contains five stages to improve the quality, service, resources of the library

1. **Define :** Define library users' needs and their expectation?

Define the better service to provide to the library users by defining the user group?

2. **Measure:** Measuring defect unit/result analysis according to the age, sex, scholarship, occupation and frequency of the library visit

3. **Analyze:** Analyze the root cause of the problem to find the better solution. In general it is toughest task

4. **Improve:** Improve the procedure and try to find out the new ideas, plans, thoughts, and ways to do better than the previous to attract the library users

5. **Control:** Control the existing systems and policies to prevent the repetition of the problems.

4. **SIX SIGMA BELT** Six Sigma follows a strict top-down approach implementing financially measurable improvement projects with the support of different methods and techniques. Specially educated employees, called Belts, are responsible for its execution. Six Sigma applies the belt system of the Japanese martial arts to determine the level and tasks of each individual employee.

The Belt includes –

1. Champions,
2. Master Black Belts,
3. Black Belts,
4. Green Belts,
5. White Belts.

For the successful implementation of Six Sigma, a perfectly balanced interplay between the different roles or belts that follow the Six Sigma strategy by 100% is indispensable. Managers acting as Six Sigma Champions assign priority projects and track the execution performed by Six Sigma Black and Green Belts, who function as team leaders and project team members. White Belts contribute with their expert knowledge in relevant fields to the project.

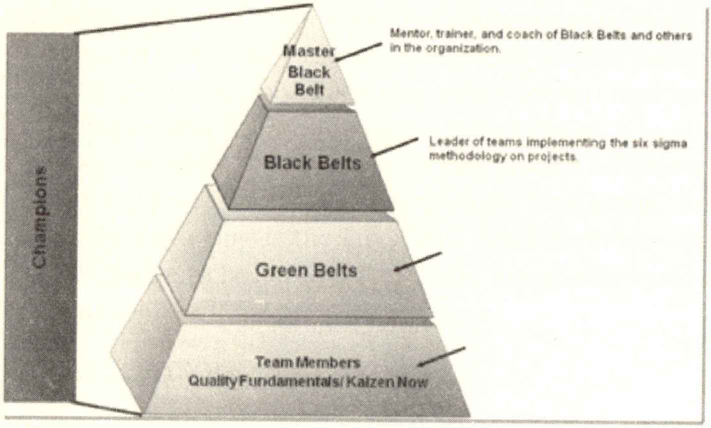

Fig 1. Six Sigma Belts

CONCLUSION

Libraries in the process of applying Six Sigma must perceive the factor that satisfies users, to develop the process and improve the standard of the library to satisfy the users. It insists on continues improvement and development of the library as well as library staff members. The ultimate goal of the library is to satisfy its users. This can be achievable by the Six Sigma. It helps library employees to have a better management to evaluate the services to library users. The planned framework and focus on process improvement are the major strengths of six sigma.

REFERENCE

1. Ahmad Ali Al-Zubi, Imtiaz Basha. (2010) Six Sigma In Libraries: A Management Perspective,Canadian Journal on Computing in Mathematics Natural Sciences, Engineering & Medicine Vol. 1, No. 3, April 2010 .
2. Chitra Koushik, Etl (2007) Six sigma application for library services, DESIDOC Bulletin of information technology.vol.27 no.5 September 2007.
3. Defeo,J.A. (1999). "Six Sigma: Road Map for Survival." *H.B.R. Focus* Vol.76. Go, Doo-gyun, et al (2000). *Six Sigma Management*, Korea Productive Center. (written in Korean)

4. Harry, M.J. Talk about six sigma. Green Belt Training Report. General Electric Company, India, 2001.

5. http://en.wikipedia.org/wiki/Six_Sigma.

8

Six Sigma Applications on LIS Field

Dolas Shobha Ganpatrao

Librarian Rajarshi Chhatrapati Shahu College Kolhapur

ABSTRACT

Now a days so many organization institutes and corporate fields using this technique and save the time loss this technique may also improve used parallel. Its services based on objectives to develop the quality and remove in our library service if we could reduce faults our serves will be improve and customer will gate satisfaction. Day by day we can take feedback for the comparison of our service, Six Sigma impact on finance return to contract sentimental and strong managerial leadership it means their is a hierarchy with fundamental strategy of leadership. The decision should be taken on the basis of wearable data authorized of primary data the decision is not based on assumption the Six Sigma used through to methods in fist 1) DNAIC- It contents. The goals of project and the voice of customer it is defined on specialist required currant data for processing to find or investigate the causes and effect relationship to acquired the routs Coues of defect under investigation (2) DMADV if DFSS _Design for six sigma it contents five steps (a) two identify to define the aims that are related the customer demand and the business strategy (b) Measure the critical to guilty that is product capability production process to find the alternatives to create a high-level decision for best utilization (c) To run the pilot study on production process.

INTRODUCTION

The Six sigma is a statically concept and it used for reducing the faults in the system to measure the faults has six stages the processes of measuring the fault after measurement in which out of these six tags contents or indicate the level of standard this technique has determined the standard of faults the processes of quality goes from one level to second level it means the faults of first level is reduced and second stages is from so it so that the fault of level is reduce and it is to be up greeted to the higher level of standard through this the object of six sigma technique is to create a process without fault in library service what are the fault it could be measure and applying the six sigma we can remove the faults in library service quality management tools have existed for a long time use is still not widely implemented services . The basic elements of six sigma are really not new histogram, run chart, failure mode and effect analysis .Quality management tools have existed for a long time use is still not widely in services sector emergence of six sigma are really not new

DEFINED SIX SIGMA

The Six Sigma related the language of managerial job. The lower line of the out put and this world gives the organizational rigorous, disciplined 'fact based path to deliver more and more profit to the lower level throw the process improvement and design project deliver by hierarchy and leaded by HIGH qualified and trended as black belts in six sigma this is creating a near complete process the product and services render by producer to the customer the services offered form upper level is satisfaction. The expectation of customer need this is covered under the six sigma project for measuring the lower line of customer impact the project completed up to sixth month and the projector used statistical tools and process improvement technique through qualified and expert workers from organization through this process it is clear that six sigma gives the shape to carrier opportunities in general practice. The six sigma works in two ways that is for the power full tools for improving process and product and also improve the process of people related and business performers six sigma is always used for developing leadership and change of management skills who adopt the six sigma concept that companies or individual or institution reach up to greatest benefit from it the coordination between people, process, costumer and culture. The six sigma changes the in site and out site outlook it also change the think , trainers training and feature leadership it's truly costumer centralized institutional.

SIX SIGMA

Use of concept -

- 1900 to 1920s: Scientific management and statistics
- Taylor and Scientific management.
- Ford Assembly Line
- Walter A. Shewhart and Statistical Process control

SIX SIGMA APPLICATIONS IN LIBRARY SERVICES

If the library service is evaluated from the user's perspective through quality evaluation tools such as Lib QUAL+, how will the follow-up process improve service, the organization. The attitude of the librarian and the process which are below the user expectation? If the improvement plans based on such evaluation are not successful in the following year, the next evaluation will produce the same results. Therefore, it should be examined how the Six Sigma theory as a follow-up of the evaluation can be applied more scientifically and systematically to the library process.

First it is essential to establish process-centered management based on the comprehensive knowledge of the process executed inside the library. Improvement plans of the Lib QUAL+ such as investment on the collection of books and improvement of the communication with the user include elements that could be or could not be defined as a process. In this study illustrations will be made that are controlled as a process. By understanding the process, it is possible to pinpoint the cause of the discrepancy between the plan and the actual result and the process to be improved the most in terms of the general quality improvement and user satisfaction. It is of the utmost importance to utilize process analysis method and Six Sigma statistical method for the successful Six Sigma management of the library.

Library is a place where knowledge understanding skill and application is discover the present sichvestion of library, is in so many problems through the DMAIC (define, measure, analyze, improve, control) we can improve the efficiency of library for solving problem arisen in the library for the solution of the problem we can adopt DMATC(define the problem the problem witch the customer or used required the exposition of the user is the first tags of our problem. We can highlight six sigma strategy on customer or users requirement .The objectives is to improve the service rendered by the library in order to make to these more efficiency to quality and key performance indicator. These are the basis to develop improved the process in library the time is most important through CTQ (Critical to quality) process.

1. Time involves the process : of user request personally and times spent on checking updating the library resources for example book, Journals, Repository, catalogue etc.

2. Staff : The staffing pattern of the library is given by university whatever the staff involve in the library technical services, user, services and library Automation.

3. Process of cost : In technical services we take loans and user services and library Automation

4. Out put : This covered over the counter transition and self service etc. (1) Staff development: we can develop the skill of the staff though education and training (2) Time and quality service: These services are value-added (3)Accessibility: The services of the book and digital library should Be available fatly and efficiently (4) Image and reputation: From the customer points of the view the status of the library projected (5)Positive customer experience: To improve the services such as laptop charging area for the user. The user may fill comfortable these all things should be interviewed by librarian the various prove being used by library.

ANALYSIS

To measure the caused and its effect if we indentify the present situation of the library, we found the short time frame for processing request sent to technical services due to lack of verification and claim is submitted by vender is manually processing so there could be duplication of the calling remedy as we analysised . The problem of library we come to no that there are sum short comings we can eliminate these deficiencies and short coming on.

1. The time of process is changed in delay and monthly bases
2. Through evaluation system we can reduction the cost of clam.
3. Through automated in puts which are based on the accessibility of library resource it could improve the statics, image or reputation.
4. Control

The controlling process should be capable for the the defects could not be recur and controlling authority should radical routs and caucus of the problem all the problem found in analysis proves it could be handily and control systematically and in sour that the condition of new process are formatted and monitoring and corrective action provided systematic reallocation of resources to ensure the process continues in a new path of optimization and ensures that conditions of the new process are document and monitored.

CONCLUSION

The plan framework or focus on process improvement are the major strengths of six sigma service industries canutliise this framework and benefit by important parameters like CTQS and KPls. The similarities among this measure across different service motivated an initial basis for services motivated to apply Six Sigma is becoming a cornerstone philosophy among the words leading corporations because it has proven itself by generating substantial business returns. Six Sigma is also seen as a great training ground for twenty- first century leadership.

REFERENCES

1. Devarajan,G.& Rahelamma, A. V., Library Compurterisation in India ,1990
2. Bauvaa, , jal.e. gaqaalaya va maaihatISaasHa vyavasqaapnaacao navao pvaah
3. Kumar,P. Six sigma in manufacturing.production journal,2002,196-202
4. 10029 Bertels 01.r.qxd 12/16/02 9.48am page 1
5. Online Journals, Encyclopedia, Wikipedia etc.
7. www.http://archive.ifla.org

9

Six Sigma : Basic Concept

Mrs. Swati Anand Marathe
Librarian, MIT MACS College,Pune

ABSTRACT

Six Sigma is the measure of quality that strives for near perfection. It is useful for Intense competitive pressures – especially from rapid globalization. Six Sigma is one of the most strong strategies ever developed to accelerate improvements in processes, products, and services, and to radically reduce manufacturing and/or administrative costs and improve quality. By using six sigma methodology (DMAIC) Define ,measure, analyse, improve and control strong strategies ever developed. Design for Six Sigma is a separate and emerging business-process management methodology related to traditional Six Sigma. DMAIC Six Sigma as practiced is usually consumed with solving existing manufacturing or service process problems and removal of the defects and variation associated with defects. A dabbawala is a person in the Indian city of Mumbai whose job is to carry and deliver freshly made food from home in lunch boxes to office workers. Accuracy rating is 99.999999 more than Six Sigma it's a case study. A true Six Sigma organization produces not only excellent product but also maintains highly efficient production and administrative systems that work effectively with the company's other service processes.The era '1986 to 1990' is referred to as the first generation of Six Sigma, and develop in third generation after the year 2000. Six Sigma can be applied to all the processes and tasks in the library. It is applicable in user assessment, library infrastructure assessment, human resource assessment, identification and categorization of library services. With the help of six sigma following elements can be studied in the Library

Key Words: Six Sigma,DMAIC,DFSS,Generation

WHAT IS SIX SIGMA

Six Sigma is a business management strategy originally developed by Motorola, USA in 1986.As of 2011 [update], it is widely used in many sectors of industry, although its use is not without controversy.

Six Sigma is the measure of quality that strives for near perfection. It is a disciplined, data-driven methodology focused on eliminating defects. A Six Sigma defect is defined as anything that falls outside of a customer's specifications. Six Sigma is a reference to a statistical measuring system, equivalent to just 3.4 defects per every million opportunities (Snee, 2003).

WHY SIX SIGMA

- Intense competitive pressures – especially from rapid globalization.
- Greater consumer demand for high quality products and services, little tolerance for failures of any type.
- Top management (and stockholder) recognition of the high costs of poor quality.
- The availability and accessibility of large data bases and the increasing ability to explore, understand, and use the data.

"Six Sigma is one of the strongest strategies ever developed to accelerate improvements in processes, products, and services, and to radically reduce manufacturing and/or administrative costs and improve quality. It achieves this by relentlessly focusing on eliminating waste and reducing defects and variations.

- Initiated Six Sigma efforts in 1992 and saved more then $600 million a year by 1999.
- Reduced time from design to certification of new projects like aircraft engines from 42 to 33 months.
- Increased market value by a compounded 27% per year through fiscal year 1998.

Selecting the right projects for SIX SIGMA

Assure that the importance of the projects is evident or can be readily demonstrated.

Assure the projects are viable and doable in a short time.

Assure that the success of the projects can be readily quantified.

1. Define

Identify projects that are measurable

Define projects including the demands of the customer and the content of the internal process.

Develop team charter

Define process map

2. Measure

Define performance standards

Measure current level of quality into Sigma. It precisely pinpoints the area causing problems.

Identify all potential causes for such problems.

3. Analyse

Establish process capability

Define performance objectives

Identify variation sources

4. Improve

Screen potential causes

Discover variable relationships among causes and effects

Establish operating tolerances

Pursue a method to resolve and ultimately eliminate problems. It is also a phase to explore the solution how to change, fix and modify the process.

Carryout a trial run for a planned period of time to ensure the revisions and improvements implemented in the process result in achieving the targeted values.

5. Control

Monitor the improved process continuously to ensure long term sustainability of the new developments.

Share the lessons learnt

Document the results and accomplishments of all the improvement activities for future reference.

SIX SIGMA – CASE STUDY

A dabbawala is a person in the Indian city of Mumbai whose job is to carry and deliver freshly made food from home in lunch boxes to office workers.

Dabbawalas pick up 1,75,000 lunches from homes and deliver to their customers everyday.Only one mistake is made in every 6 million deliveries.

Accuracy rating is 99.999999. More than Six Sigma.

Design for Six Sigma is a separate and emerging business-process management methodology related to traditional Six Sigma. While the tools and order used in Six Sigma require a process to be in place and functioning, DFSS has the objective of determining the needs of customers and the business, and driving those needs into the product solution so created. DFSS is relevant to the complex system/product synthesis phase, especially in the context of unprecedented system development. It is process *generation* in contrast with process *improvement*.

DMADV, Define – Measure – Analyze – Design – Verify, is sometimes synonymously referred to as DFSS. The traditional DMAIC (Define – Measure – Analyze – Improve – Control) Six Sigma process, as it is usually practiced, which is focused on evolutionary and continuous improvement manufacturing or service process development, usually occurs after initial system or product design and development have been largely completed. DMAIC Six Sigma as practiced is usually consumed with solving existing manufacturing or service process problems and removal of the defects and variation associated with defects. On the other hand, DFSS (or DMADV) strives to generate a new process where none existed, or where an existing process is deemed to be inadequate and in need of replacement. DFSS aims to create a process with the end in mind of optimally building the efficiencies of Six Sigma methodology into the process *before* implementation; traditional Six Sigma seeks for continuous improvement *after* a process already exists.

SIX SIGMA - FIRST GENERATION (SSG 1)

The era '1986 to 1990' is referred to as the first generation of Six Sigma, or SSG 1 for short. Pioneered at Motorola, Statistical approach,Measured Defects Per Million Opportunities (DPMO) ,Focused on:

Elimination of defects

Improving product and service quality

Reducing cost

Continuous process improvement

SIX SIGMA - SECOND GENERATION (SSG 2)

In the 1990s, the focus of Six Sigma shifted from product quality to business quality. General Electric Corp. ushered in the second generation of Six Sigma, or SSG 2 as it is known.Six Sigma became a business-centric system of management.

Strong measurement on bringing dollars to the bottom line.High potential candidates were selected as Black Belts.

SIX SIGMA - THIRD GENERATION (GEN III)

Developed after the year 2000. Gen III can show companies how to deliver products or services that, in the eyes of customers, have real value. Combines Lean Manufacturing Techniques and Six Sigma. Termed as Lean Six Sigma.Korean steel maker Posco and electronics maker Samsung has begun a Gen III program.Six Sigma can be applied to all the processes and tasks in the library. It is applicable in user assessment, library infrastructure assessment, human resource assessment, identification and categorization of library services. With the help of six sigma following elements can be studied in the Library.

Commitment towards work

Total user satisfaction

Continuous improvement

Training & education

Error prevention

Co-Operation & Team work

FOLLOWING APPLICATIONS CAN BE IMPLEMENTED IN THE LIBRARY WITH HELP OF ABOVE MENTIONED ELEMENTS

1. **Efficient Management** – The parent organization management must be cooperative and there should be continuous development of the library, by providing necessary resources like money, men & materials.

2. **Strategic planning** – With the help of six sigma for librarythere should be strategic planning which includes vision,mission,goals,objectives & strategies. This will helpful for avoiding the problems faced by libraries.

3. **User service & satisfaction** – In library the user should be the main objective of the library. To analyze and improvement

in library user's feedback is essential.

4. **Development** – Every library must have to improve in terms of infrastructure, manpower, services technologies used and work processes.

5. **Users feedback & evaluation** – With the help of six sigma tool library must have to identify users needs and provide suitable information services.

After rendering the services, on the basis of feedback the library can evaluate its functioning.

CONCLUSION

- A gauge of quality and efficiency, Six Sigma is also a measure of excellence. Embarking on a Six Sigma program means delivering top-quality service and products while virtually eliminating all internal inefficiencies (Dedhia, 2005).
- A true Six Sigma organization produces not only excellent product but also maintains highly efficient production and administrative systems that work effectively with the company's other service processes (Lucas, 2002).
- The primary factor in the successful implementation of a six sigma project is to have the necessary resources, the support and leadership of top management.
- Six Sigma can be applied to all the processes and tasks in the library. It is applicable in user assessment, library infrastructure assessment, human resource assessment, identification and categorization of library services. With the help of six sigma following elements can be studied in the Library.

REFERENCES

- Dedhia, N.S. (2005), "Six Sigma Basics", Total Quality Management, Vol.16, No.5, pp. 567-574.
- GE website http://www.ge.com
- Harry, M., and Crawford. D. (2005), "Six Sigma – The next generation", Machine Design, February Issue, pp. 126-132.

- Lucas, J M (2002), "The essential Six Sigma", Quality Progress, January, pp. 27-31.
- Motorola website http://www.motorola.com.
- Snee, R. D. and Hoerl, R.W. (2003).
- Leading Six Sigma: A Step by Step Guide Based on Experience at GE and Other Six Sigma Companies, Prentice-Hall, New Jersey.
- Thawani, S. (2004), "Six Sigma – Strategy for organizational excellence", Total Quality Management, Vol.15 No.5-6, pp. 655-664

10

Six Sigma Applications on LIS Field

Chetan S Sonawane

Librarian, KTSP Mandal's, K.M.C College, Khopoli, Tal – Khalapur, Dist-Raigad, Pin-410203, Maharashtra

ABSTRACT

Six sigma has its application in various range of processes ranging from manufacturing to service sector and variegated transactional processes. The main purpose of six sigma is customer satisfaction. Keeping consistency and doing things right is the idea behind six sigma. Success of six sigma in manufacturing sector is well known to us. But we can't firmly say about it in case with service sector. Application of Six Sigma is yet is in its initial stage. This paper focuses on the review of Six sigma to LIS field in terms of its services and its significance to LIS field.

Keywords: Six Sigma, Service sector, library services, CTQ, KPI, CSF etc

INTRODUCTION

Though quality management tools were in existence since from long time there use has been very less in service sector. Six sigma applications has enabled effective scientific management of service industries. The basic quality tool of Six sigma are

Statistical process control, histogram, run chart, failure mode and effect analysis, Cause and effect diagram and other tools that have been in existence since from long time. Six sigma offer a framework that unites these basic quality tools with high level management support. Six sigma has been introduced in the 1980's and there have been many success stories from companies like Motorola, General Electric and Allied Signal. Six sigma has tested its success in manufacturing sector but of lately taking about service sector excluding the healthcare and banking industries all other service industries has failed in implementing effective Sig Sigma technique.

WHAT IS SIX SIGMA?

Six Sigma means "a systematic innovative activity to statistically measure and analyze causes of defect that happens in all parts of management and then remove those causes." According to Six sigma defect include all causes that interrupt process or service. It is a methodology to define a problem from the viewpoint of the manager or user as a defect and ascertain its causes in order to solve it.

APPLICATION OF SIX SIGMA IN SERVICE QUALITY IMPROVEMENT

Six Sigma management is defined as follows: It is systematic and innovative activities that assess the causes for defect and errors occurred in every sector of the management based on the statistical measure, analyses the causes and ultimately eliminate them. Definition of the 'Defect' in Six sigma management include all factors that hinder process or service. Unlike the conventional innovative methodology which focuses on minimizing defect in the manufacturing venue or on the problem solving in the specific field, the Six sigma define the defect as any problem arising in all sectors of the company that is perceived problematic by the management or by the customer. Thus the Six sigma is methodologies which pinpoint the causes of such defect and eliminate them fundamentally.

As in the case of manufacturing, defect found in service incur a cost to either scrap or to do rework. Example include the need to contact again to customer to verify an order, providing an incorrect service, providing a sub standard service or even more service or even providing more than what has asked. After implementation of Six sigma in service sector like healthcare and finance have registered benefit. The length of the service is extending to call centers and human resource and product support services. Literature reviews shows that most of the applications are limited to service industries in north America and the European countries, but it is the financial benefit of Six sigma that have been published instead of discussing gain in term of process improvement. Proper identification of Critical success factor (CSF), CTQ characteristics, and Key performance indicators (KPI's) is also very important.

1. Critical Success factor (CSF)
2. Critical to quality characteristics (CTQ)
3. Key Performance Indicators (KPI)

APPLICATION OF SIX SIGMA IN LIBRARY SERVICES

Library is a place where knowledge can be found. Using this theory the present study focused on the use of DMAIC (define, measure, analyse, improve, control) methodology to improve efficiency of a local library. The following improvement steps were taken for pilot study.

Define – It refers to processes that select and control the project. Projects are defined including the demand of the user and the content of the internal process. It is the initial stage of starting the project and the most significant aspect of this stage is whether the defined project is something "measurable" or not. The scope of this study included technical service process, library automation and digital services. The tool used includes the writing of project charter.

Measure – As a phase to examine the current state of process, it precisely pinpoints the area causing problem to use it as a basis of the problem-solving. Fault or defect of the project, unit or opportunity must be clearly and precisely defined and all possible and potential causes for such problem must be identified in this step. Subsequently such problems are analyzed statistically, direction of the project and precise standard of the project subjected to the analysis must be determined. To know the different library process an audit was carried out that includes the following processes:

- Selection of the processes to be audited
- A critical examination of selected processes
- Developing the improved process

The important process in CTQ's and KPI's are as follows:

Important CTQ factors are as follows:

Time – This involves the time required to process user request through telephone, email or in person and time spent on checking, updating and shelving library resources such as books, Journal, microfilm etc

Staffing – This involves staff working in different sections of the library such as Acquisition, Processing section etc.

Cost of process – This implies the cost incurred on technical services, lending section and digitization of the library.

Output – This involves the transaction made throughout the day.

Important KPI factors are as follows:

Staff Training – Staff training is very important for the overall progress of the staff.

Value added service – Timely and quality service should be provided to all users.

Standard – Good service should be provided to retain good reputation.

Analysis – There is step for analyzing why, when and where defect occurs. The objective of this step is to characterize the project statistically and to minimize the various aspects of causes for projects. In the Library process mapping, and causes and effect diagramming were identified. The following lacunae were identified.

- Short time for technical service as per the processing request received
- Lack of verification of claims submitted by vendors
- Manual entry and processing of claim by vendors was tedious
- During the physical processing of the items there is a good chance of duplication in cataloguing as well as lending section.

Improve – It is a step to improve a few key factors confirmed in the previous Analysis process and pursue a method to improve realistic problems to be ultimately resolved. It is also a phase to explore the solution how to change, fix and modify the process. A pilot test is to be made in the actual work for the month to test the improvement plan and an analysis is to be made on the effect before and after applying the improvement plans through statistical analysis as in the previous Analysis step. After complete analysis the solutions suggested for Improvement were:

- Change in time frame to process request from daily basis to monthly basis
- Cost reduction of claims for this an effective evaluation system need to be created.
- Automated input process should be initiated as well as designing the total process based on workflow i.e. lending and cataloguing

Control – It is the step for the actual control and maintenance of the improved state. It is also a step to systemize practical plan which are selected as statistically optimal to be realistically applied, maintained and improved. All possible related problems that are specific problem identified in the analysis phase can be handled in the control phase. Control process involves monitoring and correcting action, provides systematic relocation of resources to ensure the process continues in a new path of optimization and ensure the condition of the new process are documented and monitored. This involves training of library staff and monitoring the system of data collection.

CONCLUSION

Six sigma major strength are well planned and focus on process improvement. CTQ's and KPI's are the important parameter in service industries. Libraries in the process of applying Six sigma must perceive the factor that satisfies user as an ideal quality and try to find key factors that affect quality from users' point of view. The pilot study conducted emphasis on important CTQ and KPI for various library services.

REFERENCES

1. Chitra Kaushik and Ashu Shokeen, Six sigma application for Library Services, DESIDOC Bulletin of Information Technology, Vol. 27, No. 5, September 2007, pp. 35-39.
2. Kim Dong-Suk, World Library and Information Congress: 72nd IFLA General Conference and council, 20-24 August 2006, Seoul, South Korea.

11
Six Sigma For Applications of it on Library Science Field

Prafull Vijay Mahajan
LIA, Marathi Division, National Library, Kolkata.

ABSTRACT

According to success of product benefits, future of management wants Six Sigma. Six sigma means effective and efficient tool of tools which causes 99.99966% non- defective management results. User's best satisfaction totally depends on six sigma. It is also successfully applying for IT in library. In IT era six sigma moves from traditional applications to technological applications automatically. Hence at the time of IT applications, six sigma gives result according to statistical sixth rank standard every time.

Keywords : Six Sigma, Applications of IT, Management

INTRODUCTION

We are aware about management systems & its tools for achieving the goals of organization. Sometime we use traditional management or scientific management. But according to success of product benefits, future of management wants six sigma. It is such type of tool which gives perfect management to catch the success in more and more percentage. It always shows all statistical process through analysis and reanalysis.

CONCEPT

A Greek alphabet ´ is used in mathematics which is the symbol of standard and six is such type of number which shows level/rank of standard. And now this concept is used for management. The concept was developed in 1986s at Motorola Company.

DEFINITION

According to *O'Neill and Duval1*

> Six sigma is a disciplined quality improvement methodology that focuses on moving energy process that touches the customers' energy product and service towards near perfect quality. It is a measure of the company's quality.

According to *Doug Sutton2*

> President of Fidelity Wide Processing, "Six sigma isn't just a manufacturing thing. It can be applied to the financial services industry very effectively." He also says," If you just throw technology at a business problem, all you wind up with is a bad process with new technology. If you wring out the process first, then you can really use technology to move it to a higher level."

"It always gets caught up in insatiable demands and lost ROI. Six sigma solves both those problem." Says Charles P. Costa3

Executive Vice President and CIO, at Chase Financial Services.

Kumar4 stated that six sigma is a statistical measurement, which provides the opportunity and discipline to eliminate mistakes, improve moral and save money. Doing things rightly and basic ideas behind six sigma.

A fundamental objective of six sigma is to achieve customer satisfaction and continuous improvement in processes.

From the above definitions we can say that six sigma has following **objectives**.

1. To achieve the user's/customer's satisfaction.
2. To measure the standard of company/organization.
3. To become a pillar for technology.

IMPORTANCE OF SIX SIGMA

Six sigma means effective and efficient tool of tools which causes 99.99966% non-defective management results which is proved from the below measurement.

Standard5 in statistics are as follows.

Type of Sigma	*Defect forms in per every million times upto producing an output*	*Success in %*
0	933192.8	6.68072
1	691462.5	30.85375
2	308537.5	69.14625
3	66807.2	93.31928
4	6209.7	99.37903
5	232.6	99.97674
6	3.4	99.99966

APPLICATIONS OF IT IN LIBRARY SCIENCE FIELD

We are generally aware about the applications of Information Technology in Library Science Field. Today all process happens through IT in library. In the period of traditional library, for the management of library personnel, resources and services, Dr. S. R. Ranganathan gave the basics or roots or framework for doing perfect work. But now in this information flood, we should do work with best performance way without loss of time. In this way, IT is most important part for library science field.

With the help of IT, library gives offline and online services to users such ad abstract services, Indexing services also cataloguing services, reprographic services, Newspaper, book – reading, Journal citation, etc.

Analysis

In these services sometime we are facing the problems due to Information Technology. By this way we can't give proper service/product to user. The drawbacks in IT are as follows.

DRAWBACKS THROUGH IT IN LIBRARY

1. Drawback in software.
   - Showing error- library management software or online library software or library webpage sometimes shows errors.
   - Link not found with server.
   - Low speed net surfing- Due to low speed, staff or users can't access information easily,
2. Power off- Without power, work of library may be stop.
3. Busy/deadline- sometime we can't dial proper channel due to busy/deadline or some technical problems.

METHODOLOGY

Six sigma has two types of methods/tools.

1. DMAIC- means Define, Measurement, Analyze, Improve, and Control.
2. DMADV- means Define, Measurement, Analyze, Design and Verify.

SIX SIGMA WITH IT IN LIBRARY SCIENCE FIELD

Six sigma also successfully applying for IT in library because six sigma is the such type of tools which give help to remove these drawbacks. Because it acts as antivirus for virus/error in management system. It directly attacks on error/virus of management system. For this action, it goes through proper way. Hence user's best satisfaction totally depends on six sigma.

CONCLUSION

Five laws which are developed by Dr. S. R. Ranganathan are one type of sigma for traditional library to give user's satisfaction. In IT era six sigma moves from traditional applications to technological applications automatically. Hence at the time of IT applications, six sigma gives result according to statistical sixth rank standard every time.

SUGGESTION

For keeping high standard,

1. It should use such type of library software which is creating through six sigma team.
2. Also library must select six sigma for implement the best management.

REFERENCE

1. O'Neill, M & Duvall, C.A Six sigma Quality Approach to work place evaluation. J. Facil. Manag., 2004, 3(2), 240-53.
2. http://www.cio.com/article/31999/six_sigma_for_better_IT_operations_and_customersatisfaction
3. http://www.cio.com/article/31999/six_sigma_for_better_IT_operations_and_customersatisfaction
4. Kumar, P Six sigma in manufacturing production Journal, 2002,43(2),196-202. http://office.microsoft.com/en-us/visio-help/improve-your-process-and-your-bottom-line-with-six-sigma-HA001123336.aspx

12

Application of Six Sigma Technique in Libraries

Mrs. Manjusha Laxmanrao Kanade
Librarian Shri.Shivaji Mahavidyalaya,
Mrs.Archana Khanderao Mane
Solapur University, Solapur

ABSTRACT

Previously Six Sigma Technique has been used in a Industry Sector i.e. mostly in manufacturing Industries. But, now a days it is being applied as a management technique in service sector also. The Principle objective of the Six Sigma is to achieve customer satisfaction by providing errorless and quality oriented services. The technique is based on the ideas Viz. Doing things in right manner and consistently. This paper is focussed on Six Sigma application in library services.

Keywords **:** Six Sigma, Defects, Library Services, DMAIC.

INTRODUCTION

There is need of transformation in library services. Due to the information explosion and radically changing information requirements from end users, there is need to provide timely, pinpointed and updated information to the library end user. Hence

New Management Strategies and Techniques are required for libraries.

Knowledge Management as a process can facilitate innovation for the library to acquire and store information and knowledge in the organization either internally or externally, to create and share knowledge, and to utilize, accumulate and reuse such knowledge. In short, knowledge management is a series of processes of the knowledge transformation and circulation. It should be regarded as the highest priority that the user is the center point of all processes. It is important to plan and execute new goals while evaluating and correcting errors and defects in present library services. With the help of Six Sigma method libraries can reduce level of effects in library services. Finally, the optimal condition generated by the above mentioned phases is controlled, ultimately the level of effects is decreased and six sigma level is increased.

EVALUATION OF SERVICES

To achieve maximum user satisfaction it needs to analyze the efficacy of the quality of library services. Evaluation of Quality of library services is not simply providing of library services but it also focuses on the degree of utilization by the library end users demand for information and their satisfaction in terms of quality and quantity. The service quality evaluation is based as how precisely the user needs are to be answered.

LIBQUAL+

Like tangible commodities service can not be defined and measured due to its distinctive features .Therefore, service quality is a subjective quality rather than objective one. Hence Evaluating the Service quality of the library, a new evaluation method was applied as a new evaluation measure Viz. LibQUAL+ .

STEPS IN SIX SIGMA

1. Define

It belongs to a process that selects and controls the project. Projects are defined including the demands of the user and the content of the internal process. It is the initial stage of starting the project and the most significant aspect of this stage is whether the defined project is something 'measurable' or not.

2. Measure

As a phase to examine the current state of process, it precisely pin point the area causing problems to use it as a basis of the problem-solving. Fault or defect of the project, unit, services or opportunity must be clearly and precisely defined and all possible and potential causes for such problems must be defined in this step. Subsiquently, such problems are analyzed statistically, direction of the project and precise standard of the projects subjected to the analysis must be determined.

3. Analysis

There is a step for analyzing why, when and where the defect occurs. The objective of this step is to characterize the project statistically and to minimize various aspects of the causes of the project. ANOVA and statistical hypothesis test are frequently used. In this step, the scientific verification process of the causes as well as GAP Analysis in which the discrepancy of the target value and actual goal achieved are conducted. Measure elements to be performed in the analysis step is as follows : First projects must be statistically and precisely defined in terms of the mean, standard deviation or regularity; the second the gap between the goal and the actual state in reality must be clearly defined based on minimizing variance and moving average ; Third comprehensive list of the potential causes of the problems must be produced; Fourth Statistical analysis must be made to reduce the listed items for potential causes, in to a few key factors ; fifth based on such analysis , objective prediction of the financial performance and re-examination must be made ‘ Sixth : Plan must be made for the final step of improve. To determine the priority of each project, common analysis means are used first, possibly with the palette chart. Subsiquently, more complicated statistical means are used to examine major variable causing defects.

1. Improve

It is a step to improve a few key factors confirms in the previous analysis process and perceives a method to improve realistic problems to be ultimately resolved. It also a phase to explore the solution how to change, fix and modify the process. A Pilot test is to be made in the actual work for a month to test the improvement plans and an analysis is to be made on the effect before and after applying the improvement plans through statistical analysis as in the previous analysis step. If the result is unsatisfactory additional improvement plans must be carried out.

2. Control

It is a step for the actual control and maintenance of the improve states. It is also a step to systemize practical plans which are selected as statistically optimal to be realistically applied, maintained and improved. The result and accomplishment of all improvement activities mast be made into the document and stored as the background material and basic data for the future maintenance or improvement. It should be monitored whether the constantly improving process is well maintained and developed.

First there is a stereotypical notion that service is difficult to measure due to its characteristics as a product of the service industry. Concepts such as transience and abstraction that characterize service industry might not be agreeable to the concept of the Six Sigma which emphasizes physical data of the product with accurate measurement. Second considering the characteristics of the service industry, there is no urgent need of the management innovation program since the corporate demands for internal process innovation are invested only to guarantee the market share. Third it is difficult to define CTQ(Critical to Quality) in the service sector, however it is necessary to define CTQ and conduct projects to improve it. Fourth there are more non-metric data that are difficult to analyze statiscally than metric data.

Nevertheless it is highly significant for the library to make an effort to improve its service quality. Thus efficient library management must be practiced based on the concepts of the Six Sigma management, process element and technique. By maintaining the Six Sigma quality level. Libraries can enhance the level of satisfaction of the student and professors as well as library employees beyond the usual user expectation.

PROSPECT OF THE SIX SIGMA APPLICATION IN LIBRARY

It the library service is evaluated from the user's perspective through quality evaluation tools such as LibQUAL+, how will the follow-up process improve service? The organization. The attitude of the librarian and the process which are below the user expectation? If the improvement plans based on such evaluation are not successful in the following year. The next evaluation will produce same results. Therefore. It should be examined how the Six Sigma theory as a follow-up of the evaluation can be applied more scientifically and systematically to the library process.

First it is essential to establish process-centered management based on the comprehensive knowledge of the process executed inside the library. Improvement plans of the LibQUAL+ such as investment on the collection of books and improvement of the communication with the user include elements that could be or could be or could not be defined as a process. In this study illustration will be made that are controlled as process. By understanding the process, it is possible to pinpoint the cause of the discrepancy between the plan and the actual result and the process to be improved the most in terms of the general quality improvement and user satisfaction.

It is of the utmost importance to utilize process analysis method and Six Sigma Statistical method for the successful Six

Sigma management of the library. The Six Sigma management originally used for the manufacturing industry must be modified and characterized as the process apart for the service industry. The process is an assembly of activities which convert input such as information and human resources into output such product and service. In particular its priority in task process analysis is to identify a key process by concentrating on the satisfaction of the user needs. Following is the LibQUAL+ evaluation items and processes that must be improved due to the low quality based on the evaluation result.

PROCESS CONTROL

1. Define

LibQUAL+ questions to define as a process " Improving communication with users."

AS2 : Giving users individual attention

AS4 : Readiness to respond to users' questions

AS& : Employees who understand the needs of their users

2. Measure

Measuring defect unit/result analysis according tdo the age., sex, scholarship, occupation and frequency of the library visit.

Information provided by and attitude presented from the librarians are reliable. There is no channel for suggestion from the user concerning library service.Library fails to act mmediately upon the user comments and suggestions. It takes too long to provide information for the user after the reference inquires made .Librarians are not actively engaged in collecting feedback on their service quality. Poor or insufficient understanding of the user demands.

3. Analysis

Defining potential causes for the defects, brainstorming with the personnel in charge of the process, using various techniques examining communication channels, methods and reference consultations between librarians and users. Librarian as an information expert must be active and aggressive in this dynamic interaction with the end user. Interactive communication channels must be established including real-time reference service through-,mails, electronic board, FAQ or chatting such service must be available on time and efficiently. Contents provided by the librarian must be reliable. Importance of the non-linguistic communication such as attitude should be recognized.

4. Improve

Pilot test for a month, analysis of the statistics before and after the test on the satisfaction level .Improving communication with users .Examining the gap between the actual state and optimal solutionPlan for overcoming such gap Revising strategies relevant to the regulations with careful preparation.

5. Control

Examining persistent method to improve the process, public relations for the improvement plans, strong leadership of the CEO is essential and he or she must share the vision with all the members of the company and challenge the conventional. Professional staff must be hired with ' belt system' through the innovative training programme. Human resources must be fully utilized quality control personnel should be trained and quality improvement activity should be promoted scientifically. and systematically. Master plan must be drawn.However , there is a problem that extra staff in charge of the Six Sigma process on top of the existing library task must be elegated. The six Sigma process needs champion (Chief management Head) MB (Expert on the Six Sigma Management activity),BB (active party and agent conducting improvement plan), and ? GB (support the 'Blackbelt') to define improvement objectives and process, and apply improvement plans. The Six Sigma team is to be composed of a strategy team, knowledge team and task process team that cooperate with one another for the improvement tasks. If the transference of the Blackbelt is difficult under the current library circumstances, it is possible to adopt the Balackbelt system with a dual work strategy (Managing both jobs simultaneously) that is considered more realistic.

CONCLUSION

Six sigma is an integrative management strategy with total quality control that uses statistic measure called ' sigma' to evaluate all the quality levels quantitatively, it provides efficient control environment including problem-solving process and professional training and promotes quality innovations and improves customer satisfaction level. Libraries in the process of applying Six Sigma must perceive the factor that satisfies users as an ideal quality and try to find key factors that affect quality from users' point of view. In this paper, six sigma theory is used in order to review various aspects of library management, conduct evaluation and find a quality of services necessary for improvement to raise customer satisfaction.

REFERENCES

1. Harry, M.J.Talk about Six Sigma, Green Belt Training Report. General Electric Company, India, 2001
2. Jang et al)2004) , " Empirical studies on the Application of the Six Sigma Technique
3. Kumar, P. " Six sigma in manufacturing.Production Journal" , 2002.
4. P.S.G.Kumar, " Management of Library and Information Centres ", 2000.

13

A Particular Way of Six Sigma in Libraries

B.V. Chalukya

Librarian, Shri Chhatrapati Shivaji College, Omerga, Dist. Osmanabad (M.S.)

D.E. Dadpe

Librarian, Lokmanya Tilak Mahavidlaya, Wadawani, Dist. Beed (M.S.)

ABSTRACT

This paper helps to apply scientific and systematic upgrading strategy to have a better service to meet the needs of the users and also helps to find out the solutions for complaints and problems. The theory of Six Sigma has been implementing in manufacturing sectors to eliminate wastages and users' complaint to satisfy the clients. In such a way Six Sigma can be applied in library field to maximize the users' satisfaction by eliminating their complaints and problems. In such a way this study aims to implement Six Sigma to provide better service and full satisfaction to the library users.

Key words: Knowledge, Management, Six Sigma, Demand, Users, Satisfaction

INTRODUCTION

Implementing Six Sigma we can do continues appraisal and can full fill users' needs. The eventual goal of any library is "users' satisfaction". To improve the quality of the library, this paper insisting to implement Six Sigma in library field. The principle of this study is to seek for applications of Six Sigma as a result for well-organized alertness administration. In addition it aims to launch information infrastructure and secure service in the competitive world to improve users' satisfaction. The intention of the paper is to apply of Six Sigma as a tool for efficient service provider to library users. Six Sigma will improve the quality of the library, maximizing the users' satisfaction and promote better performance.

"User Satisfaction" is the indispensable goal of any library. Six Sigma help us to do continues appraisal and improve the quality of the library to satisfy the library users in an effective and better manner. This paper is insisting to implement Six Sigma in library field. The principle of this study is to seek for applications of Six Sigma as a result for well-organized alertness administration. In addition it aims to launch information infrastructure and secure service in the competitive world to improve users' satisfaction.

QUALITY MANAGEMENT PROCESS IN LIBRARIES

To focus on customer satisfaction generally libraries are giving much attention on quality service. Quality service can be delivered if libraries improve its management efficiency. In general tailor made service will help to satisfy users. Tailor made service can be efficiently done through the process of Sig Sigma. The below diagram shows that a very first define the demand of the users then measure it , analyze the same, make in control and improve the quality then serve to users.

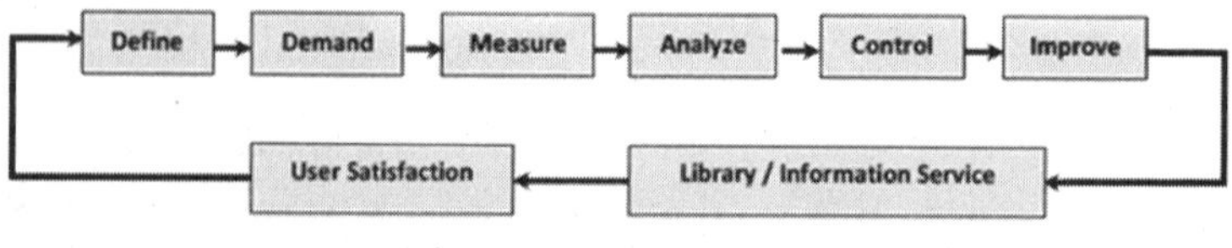

Fig. 1. Quality Management Process in Library

Library is a place where enormous of information is acquired, stored, classified and disseminated to its users at the maximum to satisfy their needs. To achieve this task library should have quality management process in libraries. So we have define the actual needs of the library users' by focusing on their demands, measure, analyze, and control over it.

KEY CONCEPTS OF SIX SIGMA

In general Six Sigma has few concepts such as Critical to Quality, Defects, Process capability, and Stable Operations.

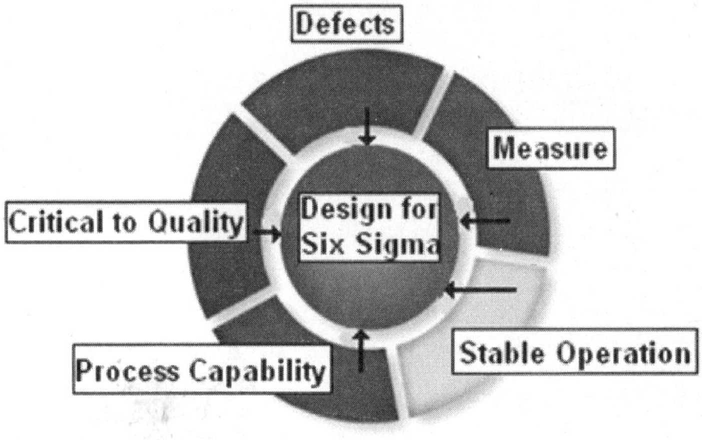

Fig. 2. Key concepts of Six Sigma

Critical to Quality – This is one of the concepts of Six Sigma which insists to have attachment with customers. In general if you have close relationship and contact with customers you may easily come to know their needs, demands and complaints. The base for the quality is to know the important and significant need of the customers.

Defects – This process helps you to overcome the failures at the same it will help you to minimize the defects. When you eliminate the defects simultaneously you can reach the point of what the customer wants.

Measure – Measurement is one of the important concept in Six Sigma.

Process Capability – This step helps you to analyze yourself to know the capability and capacity to process the delivery. Through this course you can analyze and improve the procedure to deliver your goods to customers.

Stable Operations – Every action has its own reaction. Likewise if you follow the above methods you can develop the consistency, can predict, can process and can improve what exactly customer sees and feels. The above all concepts will guide you to meet customer needs in an easiest way.

METHODOLOGIES OF SIX SIGMA.

There are two types of methodologies in Six Sigma one is DMAIC and another is DMADV.

DMAIC stands for Define, Measure, Analyze, Improve and Control. DMAIC, which is used to improve an existing business process.

DMADV stands for Define, Measure, Analyze, Design and Verify, which is used to create new product designs or process designs.

In this paper we are going to discuss about DMAIC method as this is useful to the library to improve the existing one.

MATERIALS AND METHODS

In this study we have applied DMAIC and PDCA methods. Both are insisting to have continuous assessment, improvement, and guide to bring excellent services to library users to satisfy them at the maximum. DMAIC, methodology contains five stages to improve the quality, service, resources of the library.

Define – Define library users' needs and their tone?

Define the better service to provide to the library users by defining the user group?

Measure – Measuring defect unit/result analysis according to the age, sex, scholarship, occupation and frequency of the library visit.

Analyze – Analyze the root cause of the problem to find the better solution. In general it is toughest task.

Improve – Improve the procedure and try to find out the new ideas, plans, thoughts, and ways to do better than the previous to attract the library users

Control – Control the existing systems and policies to prevent the repetition of the problems. In this stage we learn to plan to how to tackle the threat and danger which comes in the future. PDCA has four phases.

Plan – Setup the goals and objectives to processes necessary improvement for the library.

Do – Implement the processes and reach the expected standard result

Check – Study the existing one and create a new one to suit the betterment for the library users.

Act – Determine the changes to bring the betterment to improve the process.

RESULTS AND DISCUSSION

- Continues efforts will reduce process variation and help to achieve users' needs and demands
- Six sigma helps to achieve short-term rather than longterm performance
- It helps to minimize library employees work effort and maximize the users' needs
- It helps to achieve users' satisfaction and to develop the quality of the library
- Six sigma guide the employee to work smart rather than work hard

CONCLUSION

Six Sigma is generally used in manufacturing sectors to minimize the wastages and to assure the quality in such a way the same can be implemented in libraries to develop the process and improve the standard of the library to satisfy the users. Six Sigma helps to improve the standard of the library and helps to improve the skills and ability of the library employees. It insists on continues improvement and development of the library as well as library staff members. The ultimate goal of the library is to satisfy its users. This can be achievable by the Six Sigma. It helps library employees to have a better management to evaluate the services to library users.

REFERENCES

1. Antony, Jiju. "Pros and cons of Six Sigma: an academic perspective". http://www.onesixsigma.com/node/7630. Retrieved May 1, 2008.
2. De Feo, J.A. and W. Barnard, 2005. Juran Institute's Six Sigma Breakthrough and Beyond-Quality Performance Breakthrough Methods. Tata McGraw-Hill Publishing Company Limited.
3. Hamza, S.E.A., 2008. Design process improvement through the DMAIC Six Sigma approach: A case study from the Middle East. Int. J. Six Sigma Competit. Advant., 4: 35-47.
4. http://www.asq.org/learn-about-quality/project-planning-tools/overview/pdsa-cycle.html
5. http://www.sixsigmaspc.com/
6. Kim, D.S., 2006. A study on Introducing Six sigma theory in the Library for service competitiveness enhancement. IFLA, Proceeding of the World Library and Information Congress, 72nd IFLA General Conference and Council, Aug.20-24, Seoul, Korea, pp.1-16. http://ifla.queenslibrary.org/IV/ifla72/papers/146-Kim-en.pdf

14

Six Sigma Applications In Libraries

Ms. Sucheta Prabhudesai
Assistant Librarian, St. Francis Institute of Technology Engineering College), Mt. Poinsur, SVP Road, Borivali (W), Mumbai 400103

Ms. Chinmayee Bhange
Librarian, St. Francis Institute of Technology (Engineering College), Mt. Poinsur, SVP Road, Borivali (W), Mumbai 400103

ABSTRACT

Libraries and Information Centres are service-oriented organizations. Services ensue feedback which is a by-product of user satisfaction. Users of any library are its stakeholders and a satisfactory service to this user-community has always been a responsible job for the library professionals. Achieving this user-satisfaction is a fundamental objective of Six Sigma. Application of six sigma is geared toward business organizations at present and the results are rave. Six Sigma contributes not only to how ones library measures and analyzes its performance, but also to improving ones basic approach to managing the library effectively.

Key word : Six Sigma, Library Services, Quality, DMAIC

INTRODUCTION

A transformation is needed for libraries from focusing on the traditional information provider in the service operation system to focusing on the information recipient, that is, the customer. In particular, libraries are faced with radically changing user demands as well as environment changes. Therefore, new management strategies and techniques are required for libraries

In library and information centres the main aim of library to satisfy the need of its users. To achieve this goal proper library management has to follow the certain scientific principles is very important. Six Sigma is a business management strategy is to improve the quality of library process.

DEFINITION OF SIX SIGMA

Six sigma is a philosophy, a measure, and a methodology that provides businesses with the perspective and the tools needed to achieve high levels of performance for both product and service offerings (Basek and Roy,2005)

Six sigma is "a disciplined method of using extremely rigorous data gathering and statistical analysis to pinpoint sources of errors and ways of eliminating them"(Harry and Schroeder, 2000).

QUALITY MANAGEMENT IN LIBRARIE

Generally libraries are giving much attention on quality service to focus on users satisfaction. Quality service can be delivered if libraries improve its management efficiency. In general ready made service will help to satisfy users. Ready made service can be efficiently done through the process of Six Sigma. First define the demand of the users than measure it, analyze the same, make in control and improve the quality then serve to users. Library is a place where enormous of information is acquired, stored, classified and disseminated to its users at the maximum to satisfy their needs. To achieve this task library should have quality management process in libraries. So define the actual needs of the library users' by focusing on their demands, measure, analyze, and control over it

LIBRARY SERVICES AND SIX SIGMA APPLICATION

Library is a place where knowledge is discovered. Driven by this philosophy, on using the DMAIC (define,measure, analyse, improve, control) methodology to improve the efficiency of a local library.

1. Define

This is first and foremost stage to find out what is the problem, define it clearly and analyze from where it starts. This phase helps to make "problem statement". This problem statement will provide a clear description of the problems and present significant details about the problems. This 'define' phase provide to know the existing problems, and users' needs and demands.

2. Measure

The second stage of DMAIC process is "measure". The purpose of the stage is to collect data and facts related to problems with users. Measurement will be done based on data collection and analysis, mapping the process and understanding and description of the process. Data collection is one of the important processes before analyzing the situation. Measuring defect unit/ result analysis according to the age, sex, scholarship, occupation and frequency of the library visit. Measure the procedure in detail, precise the data collected to know the functionality and judge the points within the target process. Measure the available sources and services in the library. Measure the attitude and behavior of the library users. Librarian and library staff should have sound knowledge about users' behavior and deeds to serve them in a better manner and to improve library services

3. Analysis

In this stage, analyze the structure to make out the ways to eradicate the distance between the library users and library staff.

Analyze the root cause of the problem to find the better solution. In general it is toughest task. If the root cause has found then it can analyze the library users' demand in an easiest and systematic way. This process helps to minimize the distance between library employees and library users. So, close relationship helps to serve the library users in a systematic way.

4. Improve

This stage makes to improve the library condition from past to present and better in future. This phase will help the library to improve the work quick and fast. Ultimately library employees can save their time and improve their work as well as can serve the library users in fastest and quickest way. Efficient and systematic approach is indispensable to improve the library quality. This state will full fill this requirement. This phase guide the library employees to work smart rather than work hard. Ultimately this helps to minimize the work and maximize service to the Library users.

5. Control

Controlling the process, to make sure that defects do not recur, removes the root cause of the problem. All possible related problems of a specific problem identified in the analysis phase can be tackled in the control phase. Control mainly defines plans specifying process monitoring and corrective action; provides systematic reallocation of resources to ensure the process continues in a new path of optimization; and ensures that conditions of the new process are documented and monitored. This would involve training the library staff on the improved processes and also through monitoring the system such as by data collection

CONCLUTION

Libraries in the process of applying Six Sigma must perceive the factor that satisfies users as an ideal quality and try to find key factors that affect quality from users' point of view. Moreover, Libraries are made to collect objective and reliable data and employ methods of statistic analysis in order to gather data and information within the organization and use them for decision-making. As a characteristic of library service, however, there are generally distributed factors which are impossible to control or hard to qualify. Therefore, it is necessary to consider the respect that it is difficult to define problems of the current service and users' complaints.

Dr. S. R. Ranganathan father of library science said his five laws of library science fifth laws is Library is a growing organism. It is possible only librarian must thing innovate and adopt some new management concepts to library. Six Sigma is generally used in manufacturing sectors to

Minimize the wastages and to assure the quality in such a way the same can be implemented in libraries to develop the proves and improve the standard of the library to satisfy the users. In insists on continues improvement and development of the library as well as library staff members. The ultimate goal of the library is to satisfy its users. This can be achievable by the Six Sigma. It helps library employees to have a better management to evaluate the services to library Users.

REFERENCES

1. Dong-Suk Kim. A Study on Introducing Six Sigma Theory in the Library for Service Competitiveness Enhancement; World Library and Information Congress. 72nd IFLA Gereral Conference and Council; 20-24 August 2006, Seoul, Korea
2. Kaushik,Chitra,Shokeen Ashu, Kaushik Prabhakar and Khanduja Dinesh, Six Sigma Application for Library Services; DESIDOC Bulletin of Information Technology, Vol. 27, No. 5, September 2007, pp. 35-39
3. Suresh,N.; Application of Six sigma concept to Effective Academic Library Management and users satisfaction
4. http.//www.sixsigma.in/advantages-and-disadvantages-of-six-sigma.html(access on 24/08/2011)
5. http://www.col.org/forum/pcfpapers/saroja.pdf(Access on 24/08/2011)
6. http://publications.drdo.gov.in/ojs/index.php/djlit/article/viewFile/138/53(access on 24/08/2011)

15

Applications of Six Sigma in Library Science

Mrs.Madhavi Parulekar
Asstt.Librarian,AISSMSCOE,Pune

Mrs. Jyoti Kale
Asstt.Librarian, AISSMSCOE,Pune

ABSTRACT

Six sigma is a knowledge based management approach. It is a statistical concept which is used for measurement. Altogether there are six levels of measurement assumed in production management which are known as Six Sigma The main psychology of six sigma is 'customer-centric management.' Keeping 'consistency' in various jobs and 'doing things right' is the idea behind it. There is no field where six sigma cannot be applied. It is now increasingly being applied to a wide range of processes ranging from manufacturing to services and variegated transactional processes. In library science Six Sigma can be applied to maximize the users' satisfaction by eliminating their complaints and problems. This paper throws light on what is Six Sigma, key concepts, different methodologies and its implementation in library science.

Key Words: Six Sigma, Library Management, Users satisfaction

INTRODUCTION

Library is one place where chaos of activities is generally experienced. Today in the age of information revolution it is all the way necessary to streamline the operations of library. A transformation is needed for libraries from focusing on the traditional information provider in the service operation system to focusing on the information recipient, that is, the user. In particular, libraries are faced with radically changing user demands as well as environmental changes. The later can be introduction of e-resources, more specifically e-journals and books. Thus new management strategies and techniques are required for libraries. Achieving user-satisfaction is a fundamental objective kept in mind while improving its basic approach to managing the library effectively is overall objective.

CONCEPT OF SIX SIGMA

Six sigma is a knowledge based management approach where keeping consistency and doing things right is the main idea. Six sigma is also a management strategy but unlike other strategies it concentrates on reducing number of defects in any process. Other methods are mainly focusing on improvement strategies. The goal is almost same but lookout is different.

'Six Sigma Management' is defined as follows. It is a systematic and innovative activity that assesses the causes for the defects and errors occurred in every sector of the management based on the statistical measure, and at the same time it analyzes the causes and ultimately eliminates them. Definition of the 'defects' in the Six Sigma Management has a wider meaning. It takes care of all factors that hinder process or service and keeps customer unhappy.

Sigma (σ), a Greek alphabet, is used in Mathematics and statistics to define standard deviation. The sigma scale of measurement is perfectly correlated to such characteristics as defects-per-unit, parts-per-million defects, and the probability of a failure. It is a statistical measurement, which provides the opportunity and discipline to eliminate mistakes, improve morale, and save money. **As a Metrics** the term **Sigma** is often used as a scale for levels of 'goodness' or quality. Therefore, Six Sigma started as a defect reduction effort in manufacturing and was then applied to other business processes for the same purpose." Following table explains the sigma quality standard. It shows that to achieve 6 sigma level only 2 defects per billion should occur. Here the fun is all the processes are evaluated quantitatively by calculating 'Sigma Quality' standard. The goodness level of 99% equates to

i) 20000 lost articles of mail per hour

ii) Unsafe drinking water almost 15 minutes per day

iii) 5000 incorrect surgical operations per week

iv) 200,000 wrong drug prescriptions each year

v) No electricity for almost 7 hours per month

This scale reveals that in India we desperately need six sigma in all major fundamental services such as MSEDC ,BSNL, Water Supply, Road Transportation, Hospitalization the list continues......

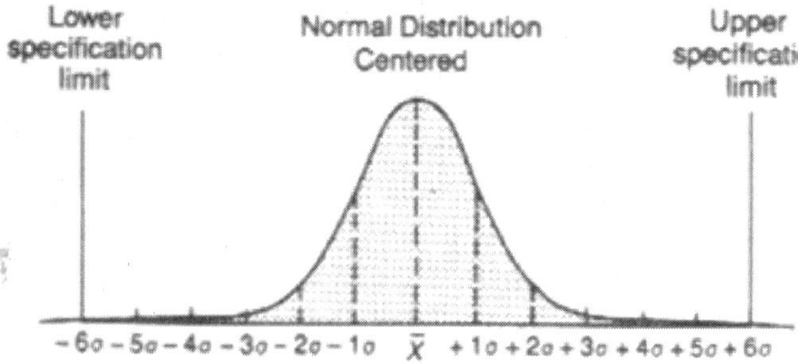

Spec. limit	Percent	Defective ppm
±1 sigma	68.27	317300
±2 sigma	95.45	45500
±3 sigma	99.73	2700
±4 sigma	99.9937	63
±5 sigma	99.999943	0.57
±6 sigma	99.9999998	.002

Fig.1. Normal Distribution and Sigma Calculations

Table1. Levels of six sigma (Breyfogle, F. W.,1999)

Specific Limit	*Percent*	*Defective ppm*
1σ	66.27	317300
2σ	95.45	45500
3σ	99.73	2700
4σ	99.9937	63
5σ	99.999943	0.57
6σ	99.9999998	0.002

This reveals us that six sigma is not merely a strategic weapon but efforts are made to put all the things in tangible form. The ultimate goal of the Six Sigma is to achieve higher 'Sigma Level'. It is very clear from the table that higher the sigma value, better the capability of the process to produce defect free work & vice-versa.

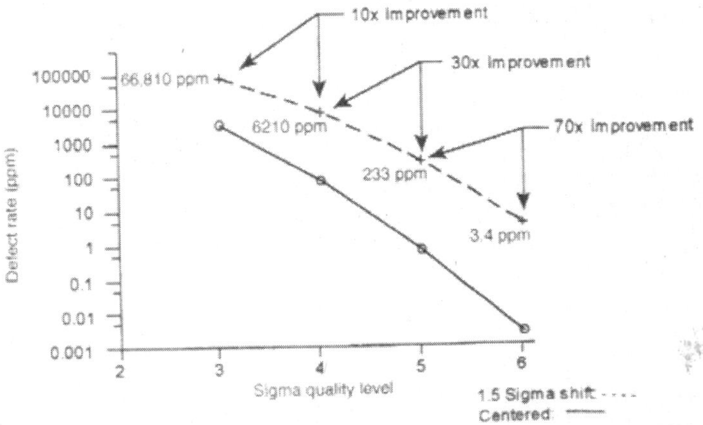

Fig. 2. Non linear relationship between DPMO and Sigma quality level.

This concept first espoused by Motorola in the early 1990s. Later thc same was implemented by General Electric, Sony etc. successfully. It has evolved over the last two decades and so has its definition. Six Sigma has literal, conceptual, and practical definitions. It uses variety of statistical tools within a structured methodology for gaining the knowledge needed to achieve better, faster and less expensive products and services.

At the heart of the methodology is the DMAIC model for process improvement. DMAIC is commonly used by Six Sigma project teams and is an acronym for:

- Define opportunity
- Measure performance
- Analyze opportunity
- Improve performance
- Control performance

It governs efforts to ensure improvements are sustained."The Six Sigma Management System drives clarity around the business strategy and the metrics that most reflect success with that strategy. It provides the framework to prioritize resources for projects that will improve the metrics, and it leverages leaders who will manage the efforts for rapid, sustainable, and improved business results."

APPLICATION OF SIX SIGMA IN LIBRARY SCIENCE

Six sigma can be applicable on five fundamental areas of library science.

1. Process improvement
2. Product & Service improvement
3. Customer Satisfactions
4. Design Methodologies
5. Supplier Improvements
6. Statistical method for the library

The process is an assembly of activities which convert input such as information and human resources into output such as product and service. In particular its priority in task process analysis is to identify key processes by concentrating on the satisfaction of the user needs.

Process Control

Define – In this step identification of areas in which six sigma applications is needed is done recursively. Feedback forms are prepared with designed questionnaire for "improving communication with users". Many times individual attention is given to users to know what they want and where the process is defective. It includes simple parameters like *'timing of library'* and 'number *of book issued'* to *'subscription of costly journals'.* However small is the problem it is taken seriously.

Measure – Measurement of reliability of defects unit/result analysis according to the age, sex, scholarship, occupation and frequency of the library visit, information provided by and attitude presented from the librarians is done. If there is no channel for suggestions from the user concerning library services, library fails to act immediately upon the user comments and suggestions. If it takes too long to provide information for the user after the reference inquiries are made, the whole process becomes slow. Librarians are not actively engaged in collecting feedback on their service quality, if poor or insufficient understanding of the user demands is there.

Analysis and Control – Once feedback from users is available and it is analyzed and the domain on which the six sigma will be applied first is decided. Once this area is decided, key persons handling users are also identified. Most of the solutions to problem are known to these people who directly deal with users. That is why in six sigma people who control the success are not top level management but middle level who are self motivated and self inspired. Such people are identified and they are called **black belts**. They are the ones who get the work done. The philosophy is these people are well acquainted with the problems and know what the solution is too. If everything (man, money, material, machines) are made available to them they are able to bring down the defects. The job of top level management is only to supply whatever black belts require as and when it is needed.

Improve – Pilot test for a month is carried out. Analysis of the statistics before and after the test on the satisfaction level improving communication with users is done. Examining the gap between the actual state and optimal solution is measured. Plans for overcoming such gap, strategies relevant to the regulations with careful preparation is devised.

STATISTICAL CONTROL TECHNIQUE

To control user satisfaction and sigma level, defects per unit (DPU) are an important parameter serving as a standard of the process which is needed to be improved. There are several processes until a final product is packed for the delivery. DPU is calculated for each process and the process with the highest DPU can be selected as the object to be improved first. DPU indicates average defects per unit, however it does not indicate the number of holes in which the defect occurs per unit.

SERVICE QUALITY EVALUATION

Service Quality Evaluation of the library is an analysis of service efficacy. Efficacy of the service quality evaluation is not restricted to the fact that service is simply provided to the user. It also focuses on the degree of utilization by the users demand for information and their satisfaction in terms of quality and quantity

CONCLUSION

The Six Sigma methodology for quality improvement is a system of many concepts, tools, and principles. A gauge of quality and efficiency, Six Sigma is also a measure of excellence. Embarking on a Six Sigma program means delivering top-quality service and products while virtually eliminating all internal inefficiencies

A true Six Sigma organization produces not only excellent product but also maintains highly efficient production and administrative systems that work effectively with the company's other service processes. The primary factor in the successful implementation of a six sigma project is to have the necessary resources, the support and leadership of top management. This paper could not cover the entire breadth and depth of this subject. The enclosed case, nevertheless, clearly demonstrated the significant impact of IS/IT on the implementation of the Six Sigma approach

REFERENCES

1. Chitra Kaushik, A. S. (2007). Six Sigma Application for Library Services.
2. Chakrabarty, Ayon and Chuan, Tan Kay.The Extent of Six Sixma Methodologies usage in services.
3. O'Nei ll, M. & Duvall, C. A six sigma quality approach to workplace evaluation. J. Facil.Manag., 2004
4. Breyfogle F.W.,Implementing Six Sigma Smarter Solutions Using Statistical Methods, 1999.
5. Brue, Greg, Design for six sigma
6. Howard S, Giltow, Design for Six Sixma for Green Belts
7. Amit Singh, Six Sigma : A Concepts & Cases

16

Six Sigma and TQM (Total Quality Management)

Kalbande, D. T.
SRF, MPKV, Rahuri

Sayed, Fayyaz. M.
SRF, MPKV, Rahuri

Dr. Shashank Sonwane
Associate Professor, Dr.B.A.M.University, Aurangabad

ABSTRACT

For decades now TQM has been a dominant management concept for improving competitiveness and financial results. In recent years, however, TQM seems to have lost some of its nimbus with other concepts and approaches such as Lean Enterprise and Six Sigma launched and increasingly in vogue. The aim of this paper is to look at TQM and Six Sigma, their backgrounds, definitions and ingredients, and their similarities and differences to see whether the two concepts really are different dishes or contain the same ingredients in different proportions.

Keywords: Six Sigma; Quality Management; TQM.

INTRODUCTION

The concept of TQM has dominated the management scene for some decades. Many organizations all over the world have tried to use TQM to achieve increased competitiveness and improved financial results. Some organizations have succeeded. For instance, quality award recipients show better financial results than comparable 'average companies'; see Hendricks and Singhal (1997) and Eriksson and Hansson (2003). However, without doubt, many organizations have also failed; see e.g., discussions in Allen and Kilmann (2001), Brah et al. (2002) and Cao et al. (2000).

Although there are several reasons for these mixed results, the failures have tarnished the TQM star and have intensified the search for new and efficient means of navigating the increasing competitiveness of a borderless world. Six Sigma and other concepts, have grown in popularity and many organizations have shifted their strategies and practices towards these concepts.

"Today, depending on whom you listen to, Six Sigma is either a revolution slashing trillions of dollars from corporate inefficiency, or it is the most maddening management fad yet devised to keep front-line workers too busy collecting data to do their jobs."

Whatever the truth is, it seems important to reflect on the reasons for this development, and try to dissect the TQM and Six Sigma concepts and analyse their composition. What is true and what is not? Are TQM and Six Sigma in fact two sides of the same coin – two versions of the same dish? We will scrutinize the two concepts, compare them and present some reflections related to this issue.

SIX SIGMA

Six Sigma: Introduction, definitions

Introduction

The Six Sigma results by Motorola impressed Jack Welsh,

then CEO at General Electric (GE), and Welch launched Six Sigma in late 1995 as one of four strategic initiatives. After 200 projects and intensive training GE moved to 3,000 projects and more training in 1996 and undertook 6,000 projects and still more training in 1997 (Pyzdek, 2001). According to Byrne (1998), Six Sigma delivered USD 320 million in productivity gains and profits in 1997, more than double Welsh's goal of USD 150 million. In the annual report of 1999 GE was able to report savings of USD 2 billion for that year alone. The success of Six Sigma at GE under Welsh's leadership is undisputed. In the 2000 GE Annual Report Welsh said: "Six Sigma has galvanized our company with an intensity the likes of which I have never seen in my 40 years at GE". The enormous savings reported from Six Sigma in GE certainly interested many leaders, who had difficulties to get TQM working in their organizations. As a result the interest in Six Sigma accelerated during the late 1990s.

Definitions

Six Sigma

1. **According to Snee** – "Six Sigma is a business improvement approach that seeks to find and eliminate causes of mistakes or defects in business processes by focusing on process outputs that are of critical importance to customers." (Snee,2004).

2. **According to McAdam and Evans** – "Six Sigma is a useful management philosophy and problem-solving methodology but it is not a comprehensive management system." (McAdam and Evans, 2004)

3. **According to Breyfogle et al.,** – "A Six Sigma initiative is designed to change the culture in an organization by way of breakthrough improvement in all aspects of the business." (Breyfogle et al., 2001)

4. **According to Pearson** – "Six Sigma is a programme that combines the most effective statistical and non-statistical methods to make overall business." (Pearson, 2001)

We can see that Six Sigma is also described by many different keywords including strategy, methodology, philosophy, approach and so on, exactly as in the case with TQM. To sum up, there is, as per above definitions we say certainly no common definition of Six Sigma.

IMPORTANT INGREDIENTS OF SIX SIGMA

There are two types of methodologies in Six Sigma one is DMAIC and another is DMADV

DMAIC stands for Define, Measure, Analyze, Improve and Control. DMAIC, which is used to Improve an existing business process.

DMADV stands for Define, Measure, Analyze, Design and Verify, which is used to create new Product designs or process designs.

BENEFITS OF SIX SIGMA

- Six Sigma helps to understand and manage customer requirements.
- Line up the key business process to achieve the needed requirements.
- Exploit accuracy in data analysis to minimize defects in the process.
- Bring fast development and continue improvement to business process.
- Minimizing the effort and maximizing the profit.
- Helps to work smart rather than hard.
- Bringing the efficiency among employees.

KEY CONCEPTS OF SIX SIGMA

In general Six Sigma has few concepts such as Critical to Quality, Defects, Process

Capability, and Stable Operations.

Critical to Quality

This is one of the concepts of Six Sigma which insists to have Attachment with Customers. In general if you have close relationship and contact with customers you may Easily come to know their needs, demands and complaints. The base for the quality is to Know the important and significant need of the customers.

Defects

This process helps you to overcome the failures at the same it will help you to minimize The defects. When you eliminate the defects simultaneously you can reach the point of what the customer wants.

Process Capability

This step helps you to analyze yourself to know the capability and capacity to process the delivery. Through this course you can analyze and improve the procedure to deliver your goods to customers.

Stable Operations

Every action has its own reaction. Likewise if you follow the above methods you can develop the consistency, can predict, can process and can improve what exactly customer sees and feels. The above all concepts will guide you to meet customer needs in an easiest way.

COMPARISONS OF TQM AND SIX SIGMA

There are few studies that directly compare TQM with Six Sigma. In the limited studies that do exist, conclusions on the relationship differ significantly. That is not, in our opinion, surprising since a comparison between two fairly vague concepts relies to a great extent on the definitions used. Ricondo and Viles (2005) compare Six Sigma and its link to TQM, BPR, lean and learning organization, paying attention to their origins, values, methodologies and tools. Yang (2004) presents an interesting comparison between TQM and Six Sigma based on twelve dimensions: development, principles, features, operation, focus, practices, techniques, leadership, rewards, training, change, and culture. He concludes, among other things, that the core values differ and suggests an integration of TQM and Six Sigma. We agree with Yang (2004) at several points.

According to Snee (2004), there are four aspects of Six Sigma that are not emphasized sufficiently in TQM. First, Six Sigma places a clear focus on bottom line financial results. No Six Sigma project is approved unless the bottom line impact has been identified. Many projects have reported saving between USD 175,000 up to USD 1 million. This bottom line focus is central to strong management leadership and support. However, it is in our opinion a bit peculiar that, in many cases, only projects referred to as 'Six Sigma projects' are investigated from a financial point of view. An investigation of successful Swedish companies revealed that the financial benefits from improvement projects related to TQM were not measured at all (Eriksson and Garvare, 2005).

The third characteristic of Six Sigma is that it sequences and links the improvement tools into an overall approach – that is, DMAIC sequences and links key tools proven to be effective in improving processes. The fourth point is that Six Sigma creates an infrastructure of champions, Master Black Belts, Black Belts and Green Belts that lead, deploy and implement the approach. Here we also want to emphasize the important role of the Champion. The Champions are not 'belts' or analysts in any traditional sense of the word. Champions are responsible for keeping the Six Sigma program focused within their business area; they select Black Belts, approve projects, set improvement targets, and provide the resources needed to conduct the projects (Watson, 2003).

Lucas (2002) asserts that Six Sigma is essentially a methodology for disciplined quality improvements. Because this is a prime ingredient of TQM, many firms have found that adding a Six Sigma program to their business system, gives them all, or almost all, of the elements of TQM and concludes that "current business system + Six Sigma = Total Quality Management".

DIFFERENCE BETWEEN SIX SIGMA AND TQM

Six Sigma	*TQM*
Executive ownership	Self-directed work teams
Business strategy execution system	Quality initiative
Truly cross-functional	largely within a single function
Focused training with verifiable return	No mass training in statistics and quality
Business results oriented	Return on investment Quality oriented

CONCLUSION

Six Sigma is becoming a cornerstone philosophy among the world's leading corporations because it has proven itself by generating substantial business returns. Six Sigma is also seen as a great training ground for twenty-first century leadership. It is now fairly commonplace for people who are well trained in Six Sigma to achieve top leadership positions.

The TQM community appears to have a reluctance to stress to novices what routes to take when implementing TQM and this is of course a doubtful strategy since the best routes differ from organization to organization. A self-assessment using quality award criterion has been described as a way to first find improvement opportunities for the organization. However, for many organizations these criteria may be too complex and as they pose questions rather than give answers, they may be too abstract. Questions of what you have done to make your soup smooth or your meal tender are fine if you are a TQM chef, but if you are not, you may end up doing nothing. Six Sigma descriptions, where actions are outlined without much discussion may thus be a fine way of introducing several aspects of TQM to an organization.

REFERENCES

- Ahmad Ali Al-Zubi, Imtiaz Basha,(2010).Six sigma in Libraries ,A management perspective. *Canadian Journal on Computing in Mathematics, Natural Sciences, Engineering & Medicine.* Vol.1.No.3.pp.86-93.

- Allen, R.S. and Kilmann, R.H. (2001) 'The role of the award system for a Total QualityManagement based strategy', *Journal of Organizational Change,* Vol. 14, No. 2.
- Basu, R. (2004) 'Six Sigma to operational excellence: role of tools and techniques', *International Journal of Six Sigma and Competitive Advantage,* Vol. 1, No. 1, pp.44–64.
- Bhote, K.R. (2002) *The Ultimate Six Sigma. Beyond Quality Excellence to Total Business Excellence,* AMACOM, New York.
- Boaden, R.J. (1996) 'Is Total Quality Management really unique?', *Total Quality Management,* Vol. 7, No. 5, pp.553–570.
- Boaden, R.J. (1997) 'What is Total Quality Management ... and does it matter?', *Total Quality Management,* Vol. 8, No. 4, pp.153–171.
- Cao, G., Clarke, S. and Lehaney, B. (2000) 'A systematic view of organisational change and TQM', *The TQM Magazine,* Vol. 12, No. 3, pp.186–193.
- Dahlgaard, J.J., Kristensen, K. and Kanji, G.K. (1998) *Fundamentals of Total Quality Management,* Chapman & Hill, London.
- Eckes, G. (2003) 'Making Six Sigma last (and work)', *Ivey Management Services,* November–December, pp.1–5.
- Eriksson, H. and Hansson, J. (2003) 'The impact of TQM on financial performance', *Measuring Business Excellence,* Vol. 7, No. 1, pp.36–50.
- Goodman, J. and Theuerkauf, J. (2005) 'What's wrong with Six Sigma?', *Quality Progress,* Vol. 38, January, pp.37–42.
- Hellsten, U. and Klefsj , B. (2000) 'TQM as a management system consisting of values methodologies and tools', *The TQM Magazine,* Vol. 12, No. 4, pp.238–244.
- Herold III, F.C., Carden, P. and Stephens, K. (2003) 'Six Sigma', *Six Sigma and Related Studies in the Quality Disciplines. The Best on Quality Book Series of the International Academy for Quality,* Vol. 14, Chapter 2, pp.15–34.
- Hoerl, R. (2004) 'One perspective of the future of Six Sigma', *International Journal of SixSigma and Competitive Advantage,* Vol. 1, No. 1, pp.112–119.
- Hong, G.Y. and Goh, T.N. (2004) 'A comparison of Six Sigma and GQM approaches in Software development', *International Journal of Six Sigma and Competitive Advantage*Vol. 1, No. 1, pp.65–75.

- Klefsj , B., Wiklund, H. and Edgeman, R. (2001) 'Six Sigma seen as a methodology for Total Quality Management', *Measuring Business Excellence*, Vol. 5, No. 1, pp.31–35.
- Lau, R.S.M. and Andersson, C.A. (1998) 'A three-dimensional perspective of Total Quality
- Lucas, J.M. (2002) 'The essential of Six Sigma', *Quality Progress*, Vol. 35, January, pp.27–31.
- Magnusson, K., Kroslid, D. and Bergman, B. (2003) *Six Sigma. The Pragmatic Approach*,

17

Six Sigma Applications For Library Services

Ajay Khatri

Librarian, SRC Ayurved College,Chikhli Dist. Buldana

Vrushali Dandawate

Librarian/Head, Central Library, AISSMS College Of Engineering, Pune

ABSTRACT

We get to find that Six sigma is applied to a wide range of processes ranging from manufacturing to services and variegated transactional processes. The Moto of six sigma is to achieve customer satisfaction. As well as observation shows that applying six sigma to services is still limited. Present paper provides a review and a pilot study on six sigma application for library services with emphasis on necessary critical success factors and key performance indicators for a project to be successful.

***Keywords*:** Six sigma, library services

INTRODUCTION

The emergence of six sigma has renewed interest in the scientific management of service industries. The basic elements of six sigma are really not new. Statistical process control, histogram, run chart, failure mode and effect analysis, cause and effect diagram, and other tools have been in use for some time.

Six sigma offers a framework that unites these basic quality tools with high-level management support.

Since the introduction of six sigma in the 1980s, there have been many success stories from companies like Motorola, General Electric, and Allied Signal. The majority of these stories are from the manufacturing sector. The service sector, barring the healthcare and banking industries, are lagging behind in applying and reaping the benefits of six sigma.

WHAT IS SIX SIGMA?

According to Harry3, CEO of Six Sigma Academy, Phoenix, USA: Six sigma is a well-structured, disciplined, data-driven methodology for eliminating defects, waste, or quality control problems of all kinds in manufacturing, service delivery, management, and other business activities It is a business strategy that allows companies to drastically improve their performance by designing and monitoring everyday business activities in ways that minimize waste and resources while increasing customer satisfaction.

According to O'Neill and Duvall4, six sigma is a disciplined quality improvement methodology that focuses on moving every process that touches the customers' every product and service towards near-perfect quality. It is a measure of the company's quality. Maleyeff and Krayenvenger5 noted that six sigma implies three things: statistical measurement, management strategy, and quality culture. It is a measure of how well a process is performing through statistical measuring of quality level. It is a new management strategy under leadership of the top management responsible for quality innovation and total customer satisfaction. It is also a quality culture. It provides the way to do things right the first time and to work smarter using data information. It also provides an atmosphere to solve many critical-to-quality (CTQ) problems through team efforts.

APPLICATION OF SIX SIGMA IN SERVICES SECTOR

Just as for manufacturing, defects found in service incur a cost to either scrap or to rework. Examples include the need to re-contact a customer to verify an order, providing an incorrect service, providing a substandard service or even over service or providing more than what is required.

Service organizations such as healthcare and finance have been implementing six sigma and are registering benefits. The breadth of applications is now expanding to other services including call centers and human resource and product support services6. Literature review shows that most applications are limited to service industries in North America and the European countries, but it is the financial benefits of six sigma that have been publicised, instead of discussing gain in terms of process improvement. Also, important to note is that the applications emphasized the proper identification of critical success factors (CSFs), CTQ characteristics, and key performance indicators (KPIs). These factors have been discussed here.

3.1 Critical Success Factors

3.2 Critical-to-quality

3.3 Key Performance Indicators

SIX SIGMA APPLICATIONS IN LIBRARY SERVICES

Library is a place where knowledge is discovered. Driven by this philosophy, the Six Sigma focus on using the DMAIC (define, measure, analyses, improve, control) methodology to improve the efficiency of a local library. The following process improvement steps were taken for this.

Define

Define the problem and what the user requires8. The define phase sets the expectation of the improvement of project and maintenance of focus of six sigma strategy on user's requirement. The objective here was to improve services offered by the library in order to make these more efficient. This required a review of the CTQs and KPIs such as process costs, staffing level, and outcome measures. The scope of this study included technical service process, library automation, and digital services. The tool used included writing up the project charter.

Measure

To become familiar with the different library processes, an audit was carried out. The audit process included: Selection of the processes to be audited A critical examination of selected process Developing the improved processes. A critical examination of the library process during the audit helped to identify the important CTQs and KPIs (Table 1). These became the basis to develop improved processes.

A brief explanation of the CTQs determined from the study have been given below:

1. Time – This involves the time to process user's requests through telephone,e-mail or in person, and time spent on checking, updating and shelving the library resource such as books, journals, microfilms, etc.

2. Staffing level – This refer to the library staff involved in the technical services, loans, and user services, and library automation and digital services

3. Cost of process – This refers to the cost involved in technical services, loans, and user services, and library automation and digital services

4. Volume of output – This includes over-thecounter transactions and also transactions using the self-service machines.

The KPIs of the study have been discussed below:

(i) Staff development: Involves developing the skills of the staff through education and Training

(ii) Timely and quality service: Needs to be value-added and proactive

(iii) Accessibility: To make the books and digital library services available as quickly and as efficiently as possible

(iv) Image and reputation: This is the status of the library as seen from a customer's point to view

(v) Positive customer experience: To improve the physical ambience of the library premises and to add features such as laptop charging areas etc., to make the library users feel comfortable.

The tools used for this phase included interviewing the library in-charges of the various processes being used by the library.

Analysis

Using process mapping, and causes and effects diagramming, the present status of the library processes was identified. The following shortcomings were identified: Short time frame for processing requests sent to technical services Lack of verification of the claims submitted by vendors Manual inputting and processing of the claims by vendors was laborious While physically processing the items, there was some degree of work duplication in the receiving and cataloguing sections.

Solutions

A complete analysis of the library provided answers on how the above shortcomings could be eliminated. The solutions suggested to overcome the deficiencies were:

(i) Change in time frame to process requests from daily basis to monthly basis

(ii) Reduction in the cost incurred due to claim. An evaluation system can be created

(iii) Initiation of a process of automated inputs as well as designing the workflow based on the total process, i.e., receiving and cataloguing.

The above improvement may also help in enhancing the accessibility of library resources, which would in turn improve the image and reputation of the library.

Control

Controlling the process, to make sure that defects do not recur, removes the root cause of the problem. All possible related problems of a specific problem identified in the analysis phase can be tackled in the control phase. Control mainly defines plans specifying process monitoring and corrective action; provides systematic reallocation of resources to ensure the process continues in a new path of optimisation; and ensures that conditions of the new process are documented and monitored. This would involve training the library staff on the improved processes and also through monitoring the system such as by data collection.

CONCLUSION

The planned framework and focus on process improvement are the major strengths of six sigma. Service industries can utilize this framework, and can benefit by identifying important parameters like CTQs and KPIs. The similarities among these parameters across different services provide an initial basis for service providers to apply six sigma. The pilot study identified a number of important CTQs and KPIs unique to libraries, and that it is entirely possible to tailor a range of six sigma tools fors various library services.

REFERENCES

1. Bott, C.; Keim, E.; Kim, S. & Palser, L. Service quality six sigma case studies. In ASQ's 54th Annual Quality Congress. pp. 225-31.
2. Goh, T.N. A strategic assessment of six sigma. Quality Reliability Engineering, 2002, 18(1), 403-10.
3. Harry, M.J. Talk about six sigma. Green Belt Training Report. General Electric Company, India, 2001.
4. Henderson, K.M. & Evans, J.R. Successful implementation of six sigma: Benchmarking. Int. J. Benchmarking, 2002, 7(4), 260-82.
5. Kumar, P. Six sigma in manufacturing. Production Journal, 2002, 43(2), 196-202.
6. Maleyeff, J. & Krayenvenger, D.E. Goal setting with six sigma mean shift determination. Air Engg. Aero. Tech., 2004, 76(2),577-83.

18

Six Sigma Applications on Library and Information Science Field

Miss. Zeenat Sikilkar

Librarian Poona Institute of Management Sciences and Entrepreneurship

ABSTRACT

This paper reviews the application of six sigma in Academic Library Management. Emphasis is given to application issues such as what are necessary critical success factors and key performance Library in order for a Provide better service to the users. The aim of this paper is to help widen the scope of six sigma application in Academic Library Management. The ultimate goal of libraries, through setting up and carrying out Six Sigma projects as well as continuing evaluation.

Key words: *Six Sigma, Six Sigma methodology, DMAIC, DMADV, Six Sigma Application.*

INTRODUCTION

Modern Library and information centers are no more restricted to books or printed material. It lays great emphasis on objectives to be achieved by the system. It's now required to satisfy the need of its users. A transformation is needed for libraries from focusing on the traditional information provider in the service operation system to focusing on the information recipient, that is, the users. To achieve this goal proper library management based on scientific principles is very important. Six Sigma is a business management strategy is to improve the quality of process outputs by identifying and removing the causes of defects and minimizing variability in manufacturing and business processes.

Various Questions arises in mind are ...

What is the Six Sigma methodology ?

Six Sigma is a statistically driven methodology which focuses on the elimination of the defects and implementation of a measurement-based strategy that leads to process improvement and variation reduction.

What is statistical representation of Six Sigma ?

The statistical representation of Six Sigma describes that a process must not produce more than 3.4 defects per million opportunities. Process sigma is calculated by using a Six Sigma calculator.

What are the costs and savings of Six Sigma ?

In order to significantly reduce costs and increase sales by applying the Six Sigma requires investing in training, organizational infrastructure and culture evolution. It will require money to make money.

What is the difference between the Six Sigma DMAIC and DMADV methodologies?

DMAIC is used for the purpose of incremental improvements to the existing processes, while DMADV is used for innovative improvements in new processes and designs. It is also called as DFSS.

They have similar first three steps(Define, Measure and Analyze) while they differ in last two steps in DMAIC it is improve and control while in DMADV it is design and verify.

ADVANTAGES OF SIX SIGMA

- Six Sigma helps to understand and manage user needs and increase efficiency of employee. Maximize the user's satisfaction.
- Line up the key process to achieve the needed requirements
- Exploit accuracy in data analysis to minimize defects in the process
- Bring fast development and continue improvement to management process.
- Helps to work smart rather than hard.

DISADVANTAGES OF SIX SIGMA

- To obtain the quality standards leads to more time spent in areas which are less profitable.
- Six Sigma gives emphasis on the rigidity of the process which basically contradicts the innovation and kills the creativity.
- It promotes outsourcing of improvement projects with lack of accountability
- Six Sigma implementation constantly require skilled man force.

QUALITY MANAGEMENT IN LIBRARIES

Generally libraries are giving much attention on quality service to focus on user's satisfaction. In general readymade service will help to satisfy users. Readymade service can be efficiently done through the process of Sig Sigma. First define the demand of the users then measure it, analyze the same, make in control and improve the quality then serve to users Library is a place where enormous of information is acquired, stored, classified and disseminated to its users at the maximum to satisfy their needs. To achieve this task library should have quality management process in libraries. So we have define the actual needs of the library users' by focusing on their demands, measure, analyze, and control over it. It should be regarded as the highest priority that the user is the center of all the processes from the initial phase of service planning to the final phase of evaluation, so the changing needs of the user are met and new ones are created. Along with consideration of the user priority, it is also important to secure a sufficient amount of information for decision making and to define and comprehend the cause based on the statistical analysis of this information. Moreover, it is essential to clarify knowledge elements relevant to the future core capacity, comparing it with the standard of the current organization and restructuring based on the result.

Hence this study aims to apply a statistical management technique and new quality management theory different from a conventional one to examine the possibility and viability of such application. To achieve this goal the theoretical background is reviewed including philosophy, key concepts and the application of the 'Six Sigma' method. Subsequently, the process is examined which enables user satisfaction improvement due to 'sigma quality' maintenance of the service.

SERVICE QUALITY EVALUATION

Service Quality Evaluation of the library is an analysis of service efficacy. Efficacy of the service quality evaluation is not restricted to the fact that service is simply provided to the user. It also focuses on the degree of utilization by the users demand for information and their satisfaction in terms of quality and quantity.

Research has been conducted on the service quality evaluation model which has been studied in the service marketing field of management studies. The evaluation factor of LibQUAL+ is the perceived difference or gap between user expectation and actual satisfaction after using the service.

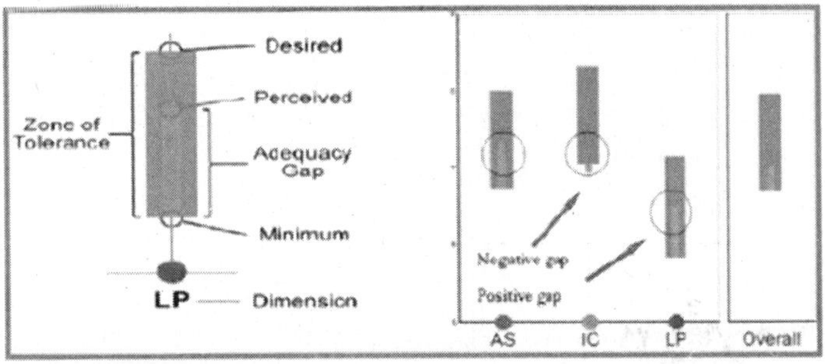

LibQUAL+ gap analysis

When a user intends to use library service, he or she is bound to have a certain level of expectation on the content and quality of the service. Users hold such expectation unconsciously in various ways and it is called 'pre-expectation.' On the other hand, user satisfaction is evaluated after the user receives the library service. By comparing the pre-expectation and actual experience of the user, quality recognition of the library service can be measured.

The user demands must be examined in order to evaluate efficacy of the library. User demands are defined in accordance with following categories: the degree of satisfaction regarding the current service and any particular demand or suggestion from the user relevant to the library objectives. User satisfaction varies by the degree of pre-expectation and actual service quality. The higher pre-expectation is, the greater the difference becomes on the service result.

Libraries are interested in 'quality management' focused on the customer satisfaction as a new management strategy for the improvement of their current 'quality level' which is fallen far behind. Quality management is an approach to improve management efficiency and resilience as a whole.

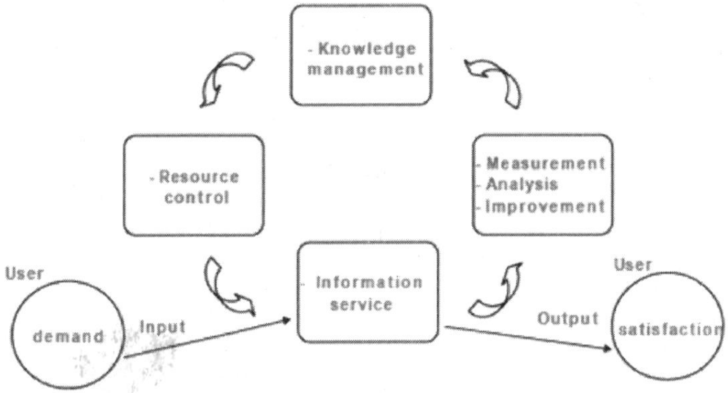

Quality management process in library

SIX SIGMA FOR THE SERVICE QUALITY IMPROVEMENT

'Six Sigma Management' is defined as follows: it is a systemic and innovative activity for the defects and errors occurred in every sector of the management based on the statistical measure, analyzes the causes and ultimately eliminates them. Definition of the 'defects' in the Six Sigma Management includes all factors that hinder process or service. Unlike the conventional innovation methodology which focuses on minimizing defects in the manufacturing venue or on the problem-solving in the specific field, the Six Sigma defines defect as any problem arising in all sectors of the company that is perceived problematic by the management or by the customer.

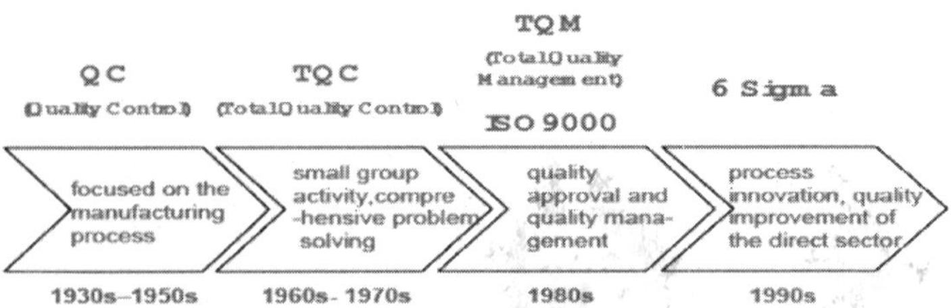

Evolution and Development of the Six Sigma

The transformation of the attitude and work culture in the organization, the Six Sigma encourages employees to work 'smart' instead of merely emphasizing hard-work.

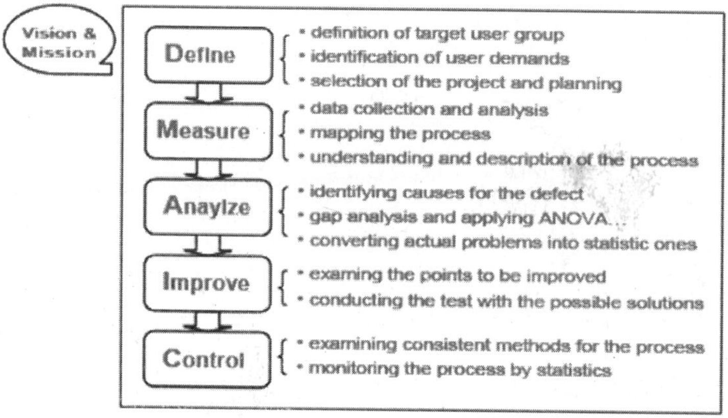

Five Steps of the Six Sigma (DMAIC)

PROSPECT OF THE SIX SIGMA APPLICATION IN LIBRARY

If the library service is evaluated from the user's perspective through quality evaluation tools such as LibQUAL+, how will the follow-up process improve service, the organization, the attitude of the librarian and the process which are below the user expectation? If the improvement plans based on such evaluation are not successful in the following year, the next evaluation will produce the same results. Therefore, it should be examined how the Six Sigma theory as a follow-up of the evaluation can be applied more scientifically and systematically to the library process.

CONCLUSION

The basic objective of any library is maximum use of it. Its also said by Dr. S.R . Ranganathan father of library science is Library is a growing organism in his fifth law of Library science. It is possible only librarian must thing innovate and adopt some new management concepts to library. Six Sigma is an integrative management strategy with total quality control. Libraries in the process of applying Six Sigma must perceive the factor that satisfies users as an ideal quality and try to find key factors that affect quality from users' point of view .Six Sigma is generally used in manufacturing sectors to minimize the wastages and to assure this quality in such a way the same can be implemented in libraries to develop the process and improve the standard of the library to satisfy the users. It insists on continues improvement and development of the library as well as library staff members. The ultimate goal of the library is to satisfy its users. The future is bright for Six Sigma programs with the increasing awareness regarding the potential benefits of implementing the Six Sigma initiatives. It helps library employees to have a better management to evaluate the services to library users.

REFERENCES

1. Ahmad Ali Al-Zubi, Imtiaz Basha. (2010) Six Sigma In Libraries: A Management Perspective,Canadian Journal on Computing in Mathematics Natural Sciences, Engineering & Medicine Vol. 1, No. 3, April 2010.
2. Chitra Koushik ,Etl (2007) Six sigma application for library services,DESIDOC Bulletin of information technology.vol.27 no.5 september 2007.
3. Thomas Pyzdek & Paul Keller (2010) The Six Sigma Handbook,Tata Mcgraw-Hill , Third Edition.
4. El-Haik, B. and Roy, D.M. (2005). Service design for six sigma: a roadmap for excellence, John Wiley and Sons, Inc., Hoboken: New Jersey.
5. http://www.iamot.org/conference/index.php/ocs/9/paper/view/1766/806
6. http://en.wikipedia.org/wiki/Six_Sigma
7. http://www.sixsigma.in/
8. Defeo, J.A.(1999). "Six Sigma : Road Map for Survival." H.B.R. Focus Vol.76.
9. The Six Sigma Way: How GE, Motorola, and Other Top Companies are Honing Their Performance by Peter S. Pande et al, Robert P. Neuman, and Roland R. Cavanagh, McGraw-Hill; 1 edition (April 2000)
10. Six Sigma for Dummies by Craig Gygi, Neil DeCarlo, Bruce Williams, and Stephen R. Covey; For Dummies; I edition (March 2005).

11. Six Sigma Concept & Cases by Sisodiya amit singh , (ICFAI May 2006), Hyderabad.

12. Six Sigma team by Rath and Strong , Tata Mc Graw Hill (2005) , Delhi.

13. Lessons in six Sigma :72 must-Know Truths for Management by Sarkar Debashis , Response (1999), New Delhi.

19

Six Sigma Applications for Quality Library Services

Baban Kumbhar
Tata Institute of Social Sciences, Mumbai

ABSTRACT

This paper deals with definition of Quality, Quality Management techniques. Six Sigma Method explained in detail. A fundamental objective of six Sigma is to achieve customer satisfaction. Doing things right and keeping them consistent are the idea behind Six Sigma. Key elements of quality Library Services are explained. Six Sigma as a goal of Library. DMAIC Methodology. (Define, Measure, Analysis, Improve control) explained.

Key Words: Six Sigma, Quality Library Services, DMAIC.

INTRODUCTION

Quality! Quality is on every ones lips these days because it can make the difference between success and failure in a very competitive world. Today quality means more than product reliability. Libraries are service organizations. Their worth is measured in terms of quality services (e. g. Quality of photocopy service, Quality of Barcode, Quality of Internet Access etc.) and not in terms of units produced or rupees earned. The main objective of the today's libraries is to provide quality services to users, so three Es i.e. ***Efficiency, Effectiveness*** and ***Economy*** are very important to each library.

WHAT IS QUALITY?

Joseph Juran defined quality **"*Fitness for use*" fitness is to be defined by the customer.**

ISO 8402, 1986 defined **"as quality is the totality characteristics of an entity that bear on its ability to satisfy stated and implied needs."**

Methods / Technique of Quality Management

1. ISO 9004:2008 -Guideline for performing improvement.
2. Kaizen -Japanese for change of the better. i. e. Continuous improvement.
3. PDCA - Plan Do Check Act.
4. Quality Circle – A group approach to Improvement.
5. TQM – Total Quality Management.
6. BPR – Business Process Reengineering.
7. Six Sigma – DMAIC

WHAT IS SIX SIGMA?

Six Sigma a quality improvement methodology brought into focus by Motorola, in 1980s. General Electric in began move towards focus on quality in the 1980s. Work out® the start of G.E. Journey opened new culture of ideas from everyone, everywhere decimated the bureaucracy and made boundary less behavior a reflexive, natural part of the culture, thereby creating learning environment that led to Six Sigma. Six Sigma is a highly disciplined process that helps us focus on developing and delivering near perfect products and Services. Sigma a Greek alphabet, is used in mathematics' and statistics to define standard deviation. The Sigma Scale of measurement is perfectly correlated to such characteristics as defects – per – unit parts per million defects and the probability of failure. Six is the number of sigma measured in a process, when the variation around the target is such that only 3.4 outputs out of one million are defective.

The central idea behind Six Sigma is if you can measure how many "defects" you have in a process, You can systematically figure out how to eliminate them and get as close to "Zero defects" as possible.

DEFINITIONS

According to O Neill and Duvall

"Six Sigma is a disciplined quality improvement methodology that focuses on moving every process that focuses the customers every product and service towards near perfect quality. It is a measure of company's quality.

According to Kumar P.

"Six Sigma is a Statistical Measurement, which provides the opportunity and discipline to eliminate mistakes, improve moral, and save money. Doing things rightly and keeping them consistent are the basic ideas behind Six Sigma.

A fundamental objective of Six Sigma is to achieve customer satisfaction and continuous improvement in process.

Levels of Sigma Performance

Sigma Level	*Defect Per Million Opportunities*
6	3.4
5	233
4	6,210
3	66,807
2	3,08,537
1	6,90,000

KEY ELEMENTS OF QUALITY LIBRARY SERVICES.

There are three key elements of quality library services.

1. Users.
2. Process.
3. Library Staff.

Six Sigma can be useful technique for establishing quality in library services

The User: Delighting Users

Users are the center of each library. They expect performance reliability, on time delivery of services, clear and correct transaction (Books Circulation) processing and more. In every attribute that influence user perception. We know that just being good is not enough delighting our user is a necessary.

The Process: *Outside-in Thinking*

Quality requires us to look at our library from user's perspective, not ours. In other words we must look at our process from the outside in. By understanding the transaction life cycle from user's needs and process, we can discover what they are seeing and feeling. With this knowledge, we can identify areas where we can add significant value or improvement from their perspective.

Library Personnel / Staff: *Leadership Commitment*

To provide quality services is the responsibility of every library staff. Every employee must be involved motivated, knowledgeable and information literate if we are to succeed. Hence all library staff should be trained in the strategy, statistical tools and techniques such as of Six Sigma. For knowing the techniques of six sigma training programs, workshop, seminars and conferences should be arranged on Six Sigma.

SIX SIGMA AS GOAL OF THE LIBRARY

When a library violates important user's requirements it is

generating defects, complaints. Defects means source of user irritation. Defects are costly to users and Library. Eliminating defects bring benefits. The greater the number of defects that occur the greater the cost of correcting them as well as risk of losing the users. Ideally, your library wants to avoid defects and resulting user more satisfaction.

Remember, accuracy is just one requirement. The goal of Six Sigma is to help people and processes aim high in aspiring to deliver defect free products and services. The notion of zero defects is not at work here; Six Sigma recognizes that there is always some potential for defects, even in the best run process. But at 99.9997 percent performance, Six Sigma sets a performance target where defects in many processes and products are almost nonexistent.

Research suggests when Customers Experience the negative results of faulty products and process they don't just sit around and feel depressed.

1. A single unsatisfied customer will tell nine to ten people about unhappy experience, even more people if the problem is not serious.
2. The some customer will only tell five people if a problem is handled satisfactory.
3. Thirty one percent of customers who experience service problems never register

Complaints; because it is "too much trouble" there is no easy channel of communication because they believe that no one cares.

In short defects can lead to lost users, and turned off users of the library tell others about their experience, making it that much more difficult to recover from defects. When taking up the Six Sigma banner, A Library will say in effect "we would like to get many of our user's related activities and services performing close to Six Sigma as we can." Keeping user happy is good for Library.

SIX SIGMA METHODOLOGY

DMAIC (Define, Measure, Analyze, Improve and control) is a process for continued improvement. It is a systematic scientific and fact based. This close – loop process eliminates unproductive steps, often focuses as new measurements and applies new methodology for improvements.

Define

The first step sets the stage for the project as a whole and often poses the greatest challenge to Library team. The Library team must think. Who is the user of the Library? What are the user requirements? How is the work currently being done? What are the benefits of making improvement? The first step is the figure out what a defect would be because Six Sigma is aimed at reducing defects.

Measure

The next step is to collect data to find out why, how and how often this defect occurs. Defects must be clearly, precisely defined and possible causes must be identified, and such problems are analyzed statistically. Sigma measures is looking how well or poorly your Library meeting users requirements.

Analysis

The Library team uses the analysis step to find our root cause of a problem / evident, one of the principles of good DMAIC problem solving is to consider many types of causes.

Methods

The procedure used in doing the Library work. e. g. books circulation system, manually or computerized.

Machine

The technology such as computer, printer, copier, bar code reader RFID reader, scanner etc. e.g. copier machine not working properly. RFID check In-checkout of item not working properly,

Internet access slow / not access.

Materials

Faulty data entry of books, journals, reports etc. in the Library Software. e. g. Title, Author, Class No. Price, Cost, Source, Date, Copies etc.

Measures

Faulty data, resulting from measuring a process what measured and how. Lastly analyze data using advanced statistical techniques and confirm the **"Vital View"** determents of the library performance.

IMPROVE

It is a step to improve key factors, confirmed in the analysis process for achieving good result. It is also a phase of elimination mistakes i.e. correct data entry in the Library software; correct data entry will give correct results. For the improvement of Library services, once new idea are developed, they have to be tested refined, and implemented. For the improvement of your Library you can implement best practices given by National Assessment and Accreditation Council, (NAAC) Implementation of NAAC best practices is not "Just do it" DMAIC solutions have to be carefully managed and tested; Data must be gathered to make and verify the impact of NAAC best practices. We will found defects are reduced and users are better served.

CONTROL

Controlling the Library process, to make sure that defects do not reoccur, remove the root cause of the problem. Control mainly defines Library plans, specifying process monitoring and corrective action. Thus Library team must be practiced on the concept of Six Sigma management process element and techniques, by maintaining Six Sigma quality level. Libraries can enhance satisfaction level of students and professors beyond usual user expectation.

CONCLUSION:

Six Sigma is a smarter way to manage your library. Six Sigma puts user first facts and data to drive better solution. Achieving the goal of Six Sigma requires more than small incremental improvements. It requires breakthrough in every area of Library operation. Six Sigma is a system of library management to achieve world class performance.

REFERENCES

1. Dharmadhikari Shripad: Six Sigma for Quality Management, Daily Sakal (Pune)15/12/2009
2. Dharmadhikari Shripad: Six Sigma for Quality Management, Daily Sakal (Pune)08/12/2009
3. Kaushik Chitra, Shokeen Ashu, Kaushik Probhakar, Khanduja Dinesh: Six Sigma Application for Library Services, DESIDOC Bulletin of Information Technology, 2007, 27 (5)
4. Kim Dong Suk : A study on Introducing Six Sigma Theory in the Library for Service Competitiveness Enhancement, World Library and Information Congress; 72 nd General Conference and Council, IFLA, 2006, Seoul
5. Pande Pete, Holpp Larry: What is Six Sigma? Tata McGraw Hill, New Delhi, 2006.
6. Thawani Sunil: Six Sigma Quality in Service Industry www. qualitywaves.com Accessed on 25/12/2009.
7. Smith Kennedy: Case study: Improving Customer Service with Six Sigma www Quality Digest.com accessed 25/12/2009

20

Application of Six Sigma for Library Management

Ms. Priti Dharmik

UGC Major Research Project Fellow, DLISc, RTMNU, Nagpur

Dr. Mangala. A. Hirwade

Assistant Professor, DLISc, RTMNU, Nagpur

ABSTRACT

There are so many recent management techniques used in Library and Information Science field for knowledge management. Six Sigma is one of them. Six Sigma means a systematic innovative activity to statistically measure and analyze causes of defects that happen in all parts of management, and then remove those causes. It is a methodology to define a problem from the viewpoint of managers or users as a defect and ascertain its causes in order to solve it. This study is not only to do a simple quantitative analysis to evaluate library service but also to find out user complaint factors and reduce them. In this regard, this study intends to identify the application plans of Six Sigma and its significance in the library field.

Libraries in the process of applying Six Sigma must perceive the factor that satisfies users as an ideal quality and try to find key factors that affect quality from user's point of view. This paper provides a review on six sigma application for library with emphasis on meaning, where can Six Sigma be applied, Steps of Six Sigma (DMAIC - define, measure, analyze, improve, control), Sigma Level, Sigma Scale, it is Service Quality Improvement tool, and application of six sigma in services sector. Six Sigma theories is used in order to review various aspects of library management, conduct evaluation and find a service process necessary for improvement to raise user satisfaction through setting up. In addition, it suggests what should be done in the future in association with strategies and visions for library management.

***Keywords*:** DMAIC, CSFs, CTQ, KPIs, DPMO

INTRODUCTION

Libraries are faced with radically changing user demands as well as environment changes. Thus new management strategies and techniques are required for libraries. The emergence of Six Sigma has renewed interest in the scientific management of service industries.

Since the introduction of Six Sigma in the 1980s, there have been many success stories from companies like Motorola, General Electric, and Allied Signal. The service sector, barring the healthcare and banking industries, are lagging behind in applying and reaping the benefits of Six Sigma.

Six Sigma concepts have grown in popularity and many organizations have shifted their strategies and practices towards this concept. Six Sigma is a program aimed at the near elimination of defects from every product, process, and transaction. Here present some reflections related to this issue.

SIX SIGMA

Six sigma is a measurement scale upon which improvement / performance can be gauged or overall methodology that provides standardized problem-solving tools improvement.

Sigma (σ), a Greek alphabet, is used in mathematics and

statistics to define standard deviation. The sigma scale of measurement is perfectly correlated to such characteristics as defects-per-unit, parts-per-million defects, and the probability of a failure. Six is the number of sigma measured in a process, when the variation around the target is such that only 3.4 outputs out of one million are defective. Coronado and Antony has pointed that six sigma methodologies have recently gained wide popularity because six sigma has proved to be successful not only at improving quality but also at large cost savings along with these improvements. So, an organization needs to adopt smarter six sigma solutions that are linked to bottom line benefits. (Chitra Kaushik, 2007)

GENERAL UNDERSTANDING

- Six Sigma was first developed by: Mr. Bill Smith, Motorola in 1986
- Key to the success of Six Sigma
- Process knowledge and knowledge in selection
- Top Management Commitment
- Strong Review Mechanism
- Six Sigma Improvement Process structure adopted: DMAIC
- Six Sigma is all about reducing & eliminating wastes in all processes.
- Objective of Six Sigma is to operate all measurable outcomes of the processes at "Six Sigma level" and attribute outcomes of the processes at "Zero Defect."
- Key to achieving Six Sigma Level is "Process knowledge, correct selection, application of tool and innovative solutions in improving the process"
- Six sigma is the estimated Part to Part variation at 99.99%

APPLIED SECTORS

Six Sigma can be applied the following different sectors.

1. Production

2. Design
3. Service Sector
4. Purchase
5. Human Resource Management
6. Administration
7. Quality Department
8. Management
9. Information Technology

DEVELOPMENT OF SIX SIGMA

The concept of 'defect,' the Six Sigma is distinguished from QC, TQC and TQM. The major difference of the Six Sigma from the existing quality improvement movements is the fundamental elimination of the possibility of defects. It aims to eliminate defects from the very beginning. In the Six Sigma all the processes are evaluated quantitatively and it is required to calculate 'Sigma Quality' standard. (Kim, 2006)

Development of Six Sigma has been going through mainly four stages–

1. Quality Control (QC): focused on the manufacturing process
2. Total Quality Control (TQC): small group activity, comprehensive problem solving
3. Total Quality Management (TQM): quality approval and quality management
4. Six Sigma (6 ´): quality innovation based on the statistics and systematically conducts personnel training and quality improvement activities as a management strategy.

SIGMA LEVEL

On the basis of different sigma levels library or other service sectors are improve their quality. Six Sigma identifies six levels for its successful implementation.

1. Executive Leadership
2. Champions
3. Master Black Belts
4. Black Belts
5. Green Belts
6. Yellow Belts

APPLICATION OF SIX SIGMA IN SERVICE SECTOR

Service organizations such as library, call centers and human resource and product support services have been implementing six sigma and are registering benefits. The breadth of applications is now expanding to other services including Important to note is that the applications emphasized the proper identification of critical success factors (CSFs), critical to quality (CTQ) characteristics, and key performance indicators (KPIs). These factors have been discussed here. (Chitra Kaushik, 2007)

1. Critical Success Factors
2. Critical-to-quality Characteristics
3. Key Performance Indicators

CTQs determined from the study have been given below:

1. Time
2. Staffing level
3. Cost of process
4. Volume of output

The KPIs of the study have been discussed below:

1. Staff development
2. Timely and quality service
3. Accessibility
4. Image and reputation
5. Positive customer experience

SERVICE QUALITY IMPROVEMENT TOOL

Six Sigma is a tool for measuring the quality of library services and it is suitable for the new library environment. Six Sigma Management is a systemic and innovative activity that assesses the causes for the defects and errors occurred in every sector of the management based on the statistical measure, analyze the causes and ultimately eliminate them. Definition of the 'defects' in the Six Sigma Management includes all factors that hinder process or service. Unlike the conventional innovation methodology which focuses on minimizing defects in the manufacturing venue or on the problem-solving in the specific field, the Six Sigma defines defect as any problem arising in all sectors of the company that is perceived problematic by the management or by the customer. Thus the Six Sigma is a methodology that thoroughly pinpoints the causes of such defects and eliminates them fundamentally.

LIBRARY SERVICES AND IMPLEMENTATION OF SIX SIGMA STEPS

Library is a place where knowledge is discovered. Driven by this philosophy, six sigma focused on using the DMAIC (define, measure, analyze, improve, control) methodology to improve the efficiency of library. The following steps were taken for this methodology. (Rallabandi Srinivasu, 2010)

Define – Define the problem and what the user requires. The define phase sets the expectation of the improvement of project and maintenance of focus of six sigma strategy on user's requirement. The objective here was to improve services offered by the library in order to make these more efficient. This required a review of the CTQs and KPIs such as process costs, staffing level, and outcome measures. The scope of this study included technical service process, library automation, and digital services. The tool used included writing up the project charter.

Measure – To become familiar with the different library processes, an audit was carried out. The audit process included:

- Selection of the processes to be audited
- A critical examination of selected process
- Developing the improved processes.

Analyze – Using process mapping, and causes and effects diagramming, the present status of the library processes was identified. The following shortcomings were identified:

- Short time frame for processing requests sent to technical services
- Lack of verification of the claims submitted by vendors
- Manual inputting and processing of the claims by vendors was laborious
- While physically processing the items, there was some degree of work duplication in the receiving and cataloguing sections.

Improve – The solutions suggested to overcome the deficiencies were:

- Change in time frame to process requests from daily basis to monthly basis
- Reduction in the cost incurred due to claim. An evaluation system can be created
- Initiation of a process of automated inputs as well as designing the workflow based on the total process, i.e., receiving and cataloguing.

The above improvement may also help in enhancing the accessibility of library resources, which would in turn improve the image and reputation of the library.

Control – Controlling the process, to make sure that defects do not recur, removes the root cause of the problem. All possible related problems of a specific problem identified in the analysis phase can be tackled in the control phase. Control mainly defines plans specifying process monitoring and corrective action; provides systematic reallocation of resources to ensure the process continues in a new path of optimization; and ensures that conditions of the new process are documented and monitored.

This would involve training the library staff on the improved processes and also through monitoring the system such as by data collection.

CONCLUSION

This paper explores the idea about contribution of Six Sigma in the service sector particularly library. The purpose of this paper has been to better understand different aspects of Six Sigma. It is a way of planning, organizing and understanding each activity, and of removing all the wasted effort that is routinely spent in organizations. The study identified a number of important CTQs and KPIs unique to libraries, and that it is entirely possible to tailor a range of six sigma tools for various library services. After the CTQ is selected, DMAIC steps are performed in accordance with the Six Sigma promotion strategy. Six Sigma concepts can be successfully use in order to review various aspects of library management, conduct evaluation and find a service process necessary for improvement to raise customer satisfaction.

REFERENCES

1. Chitra Kaushik, A. S. (2007). *Six Sigma Application for Library Services.* Karnal. Available at: (Accessed on 2 August 2011)
2. Kim, D.-S. (2006). *A Study on Introducing Six Sigma Theory in the Library for Service Competitiveness Enhancement.* Korea: Paiknam Academic Information Center & Library. Available at http://archive.ifla.org/IV/ifla72/papers/146-Kim-en.pdf(Accessed on 1 August 2011)
3. Rallabandi Srinivasu, G. S. (2010). *The Contributions of TQM and Six SIGMA in the Organizations to Achieve the Success in Terms of Quality.* Hyderabad, India: International Journal of Computer Applications. Available at: http://www.ijcaonline.org/volume8/number4/pxc3871704.pdf (Accessed on 1 August 2011)
4. Service Quality Improvement tool. Available at: http://www.acmainfo.com/six-sigma/Six-Sigma_Tools.pdf (Accessed on 7August 2011) Six Sigma. Available at:http://www.sixsigmais.com/sixsigmaconcept.htm (Accessed on 2 August 2011)
5. Wikipedia. *Sigma level.* Available at: http://en.wikipedia.org/wiki/Six_Sigma(Accessed on 1August 2011)
6. Wikipedia. *Sigma scale.* Available at: http://en.wikipedia.org/wiki/Six_Sigma(Accessed on 1August 2011)

21

Six Sigma Applications on LIS Field

Noorjahan A. Shaikh

Librarian, Abeda Inamdar Jr.College, Azam Campus, Camp, Pune 411001

ABSTRACT

In library and Information Centers the foremost objective is to satisfy the need of its users. Users are the backbones of library and they are the best judges to evaluate the service and the quality of the Library. To develop the library and to provide maximum users satisfaction, it is necessary to implement Six Sigma in Libraries. The theory of Six Sigma has been implementing in manufacturing sectors to eliminate wastages and users complaint to satisfy the clients. In such a way Six Sigma can be applied in Library Field to maximize the users' satisfaction by eliminating their complaints and problems. This paper helps to understand what is Six Sigma, key concepts of Six Sigma, different methodologies of Six Sigma and implementation roles of Six Sigma. Also the aim of this paper is to implement Six Sigma to provide better service and full satisfaction to the Library users. This study set out to draw and implement scientific and systematic improvement plans for a service area that failed to meet its goal or caused users' complaints.

Keywords : Six Sigma, Library management, Users' satisfaction

INTRODUCTION

This eventual goal of any library is "Users' satisfaction." The purpose of any library is to be pleased to all customers needs. Users are the backbone of library and are the best judges to evaluate the service and the quality of the Library. But in general it is difficult to satisfy completely and totally of every customer needs. To evaluate 'users' satisfaction' and to develop the quality of the library, it is mandatory to bring a new innovation. Through implementing Six Sigma we can do continues appraisal and can full fill users' needs. Six Sigma will improve the quality of the library, maximizing the users' satisfaction and promote better performance.

WHAT IS SIX SIGMA?

The term 'Six Sigma' comes from a field of statistics known as process capability studies. Originally, it referred to the ability of manufacturing process to produce a very high proportion of output within specification. Six Sigma originated as a set of practices designed to improve manufacturing process and eliminate defects. In Six Sigma, a defect is defined as any process output that does not meet customer specifications.

DEFINITION

Six Sigma is "a disciplined method of using extremely rigorous data gathering and statistical analysis to pinpoint sources of errors and ways of eliminating them." (Harry and Schroeder 2000)Six Sigma is uniquely driven by close understanding of customer needs, disciplined use of facts, data and statistical analysis and diligent attention to managing, improving and reinventing.In simple words we can say Six Sigma is a quality improvement.

BENEFITS OF SIX SIGMA

- Six Sigma helps to understand and manage customer requirements.

- Minimizing the effort and maximizing the profit.
- Helps to work smart rather than hard.
- Bringing the efficiency among employees.

KEY CONCEPTS OF SIX SIGMA

In general Six sigma has few concepts such as Critical to Quality, Defects, Process Compatibility and Stable Operations.

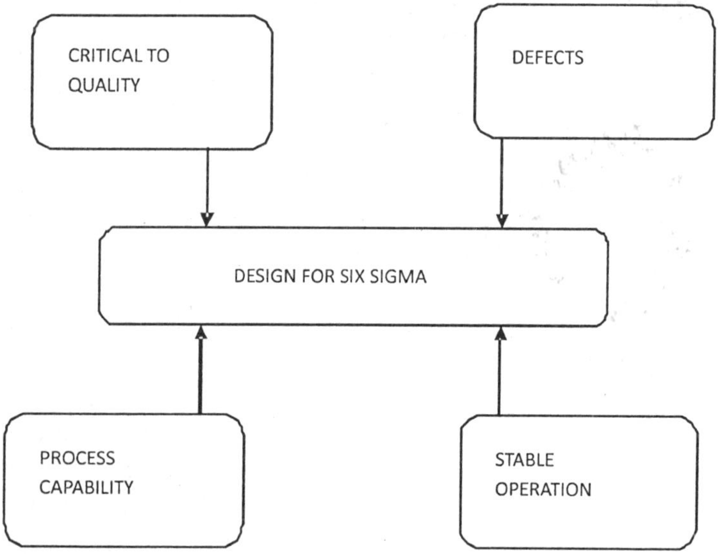

Critical to Quality – This is one of the concepts of Six Sigma which insists to have attachment with customers. The base for the quality is to know the important and significant need of the customers.

Defects – When you eliminate the defects simultaneously you can reach the point of what the customers wants.

Process Capability – This step helps you to analyze yourself to know the capability and capacity to process the delivery.

Stable Operations – By following the above methods you can develop the consistency, can predict, can process and can improve what exactly customer sees and feels.

IMPLEMENTATION ROLES

Six Sigma relies heavily on teams of people working together, not on individual effort. Six Sigma identifies several key roles for its successful implementation.

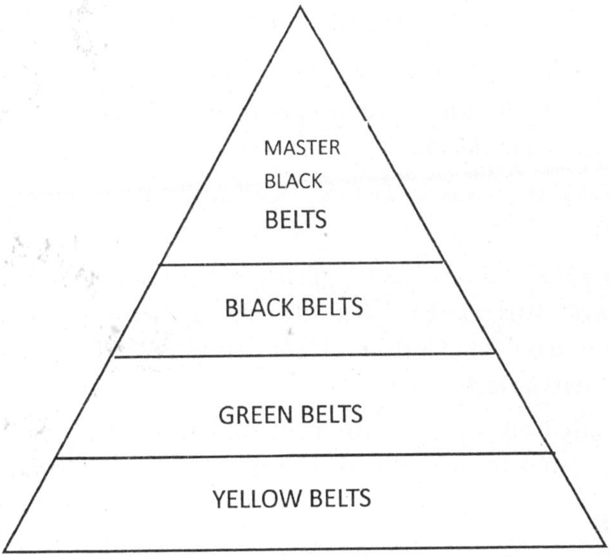

Executive Leadership – It includes the CEO and other members of top management. They are responsible for setting up a vision for Six Sigma implementation.

Champions – they take responsibility for Six Sigma implementation across the organization in an integrated manner.

Master Black Belts – They devote 100% of their time to Six Sigma. They assist champions and guide Black Belts and Green Belts.

Black Belts – They operate under Master Black Belts to apply Six Sigma methodology to specific projects.

Green Belts – They are the employers who take up Six Sigma implementation along with their other job responsibilities, operating under the guidance of Black Belts.

Yellow Belts – They represent everyone else on the team. Yellow Belts are the members, administrators, operations personnel and anyone else who might play a role.

METHODOLOGIES OF SIX SIGMA

There are two types of methodologies in Six Sigma.

DMAIC (Define, Measure, Analyze, Improve, Control)

DMADV (Define, Measure, Analyze, Design, Verify)

As DMAIC is the most suitable methodology to LIS field, we will discuss it in detail.

DMAIC stands for Define, Measure, Analyze, Improve and Control.

DEFINE : It belongs to a process that selects and controls the project. This phase helps us to make 'problem statement'. We have to find out what is the problem, define it clearly and analyze from where it starts.

Based on users requirement we can define and set the objectives and goals to meet their needs.

DEFINE

- Definition of target user group
- Identification of user demand
- Definition of better library services
- Selection of the project and planning
- Definition of forthcoming and existing problems of the library users.

MEASURE

Defining the problem is just the beginning. Next comes the most time – consuming part of the DMAIC methodology; which is accomplished by making measurements and collecting data.

Data collection is one of the important process before analyzing the situation. Measurement will be done based on data collection and analysis, mapping the process and understanding the description of the process. We can measure the available sources and services , measure the attitude and behavior of the library users.

When a user intends to use library service, he or she is bound to have a certain level of expectation on the quality of the service, even if the aspects or types of such expectation might vary among individuals. Users hold such expectation unconsciously in various ways and it is called as 'pre-expectation'. It exists prior to the actual experience of the library service. On the other hand, user satisfaction is evaluated after the user receives the library service. By comparing the pre-expectations and actual experience of the user, quality recognition of the library service can be measured.

- Data collection and analysis
- Mapping and process
- Understanding and description of the process
- Users' attitude and behavior
- Measurable and achievable

ANALYZE – You must analyze the data using powerful mathematics and statistical tools. By analyzing, you get a clear picture of the variation in your process and how to limit it. In this step the scientific variations process of the causes as well as Gap Analysis in which the discrepancy of the target value and the actual goal achieved are conducted.

In general it is toughest task. This process helps to minimize the distance between library staff and library users. So, close relationship helps to serve the library users in a systematic way.

ANALYZE

- Identifying causes for the defect
- Gap analysis
- Converting actual problems into statistic ones.
- Eliminating distance between users and library staff
- Library users demands in a systematic way.

IMPROVE: It is a step or phase to explore the solution, how to change, fix and modify the process. This phase guide to work smart rather than work hard.

This stage makes to improve the library condition from past to present and help us to do better in future. We can improve the procedure and try to find out the new ideas, plans, thoughts and ways to do better than the previous to attract the library users. This helps to maximize service to the library users.

IMPROVE

- Examining the points to be improved.
- Conducting the test with the possible solutions.
- Smart work
- To find out new ideas, plans etc.
- Current performance by reducing and removing the defects.

CONTROL – It is a step for the actual control and maintenance of the improved states. To make sure a solution can be sustained over the long term, control planning is required. Here it is mandatory to determine the effectiveness, process and implementations. It is a step to control the existing systems and policies to prevent the repetition of the problems.

This process guides us to learn to control and eliminate the library users' complaints. This stage helps us to improve the efficiency of library employees.

IMPACT OF SIX SIGMA ON LIBRARY

Six Sigma is insisting to have continuous assessment, improvement and guide to bring excellent services to library users to satisfy them at the maximum. Applying Six Sigma applications means defining the user group, users' needs and their tone, we will able to give better service to the library users. By measuring defect according to the age, sex, scholarship, occupation and frequency of the library visit we can analyze the root cause solution. By improving the plans, thoughts and ways to do better than previous we can attract the library users and also we learn to plan to how to tackle the threat and danger which comes in the future.

CONCLUSION

Six Sigma is an integrative management strategy with total quality control that uses statistic measure called 'sigma' to evaluate process, determines priority of the quality improvement activities and efficiently controls the process according to the priority.

Focused on the LIS Field, opinions of the user can be recorded through a user survey or library environment analysis and subsequently internal capacity can be accessed. The vision of the library can be shared by all members and put into practice in daily routine. The ultimate goal must be the change of the perception on library value management and enhancement of the user satisfaction through a constant quality control.

Libraries in the process of applying Six Sigma must perceive the factor that satisfies users as an ideal quality and try to find key factors that affect quality from users, point of view. As a characteristic of library service, however, there are generally distributed factors which are impossible to control or hard to quantify. Therefore, it is necessary to consider the respect that it is difficult to define problems of the current service and users' complaints. Accordingly, in drawing and implementing improvements plans, it is needed to separately prepare a process modeling for the field of library management, which is different from general manufacturing. In addition, it suggests reviewing various aspects of library management, conducting evaluation and finding a service process necessary for improvement to raise customer satisfaction. This can be achievable by the Six Sigma.

REFERENCES

- Kim, D.S.,2006. A study on Introducing Six Sigma theory in the Library for service competitiveness enhancement. IFLA, Proceeding of the world library and Information Congress, 72nd IFLA General Conference and Council, Aug.20-24; Seoul, Korea, pp : http://ifla.queenslibrary.org/IV/

ifla72/papers/146-Kim-en.pdf

- Ahmad Ali Al-Zubi, Imtiaz Basha(2010) Six Sigma In Libraries : A management perspective, Canadian Journal on Computing in Mathematics Natural Sciences, Engineering and Medicine Vol.1,No.3, April 2010
- Suresh, N. : Application of Six Sigma concept to effective Academic Library management and users satisfaction.
- Kim,Dong Suk (2006) A study on the Service quality evaluation of University Library applying the LibQUAL+. Ewha Womans University Department Of Library and information Science a masters thesis.
- Chitra, Koushik, Etl (2007) Six sigma application for library services, DESIDOC Bulletin of information technology. Vol.27, No.5, September 2007
- http://en.wikipedia.org/wiki/six sigma
- http:// Ezine Articles.com/3089819
- http:// www.sixsigmaspc.com/six-sigma/sixsigma.html.

APPLICATION OF INFORMATION TECHNOLOGY ON LIBRARY SERVICES

22

Building E-resource in Digital Library in Engineering Colleges : An Overview

Mahendra K. Sahu
Librarian Gandhi Institute Management Studies (GIMS), Gunupur, Orisa
Dr. R. K. Mahapatra
Principal, College of Library and Information Science.

ABSTRACT

Libraries have witnessed a great metamorphosis in recent years both in their collection and development and in their service structure. Over the last several years, a significant transformation has been noticed in collection development policies and practices; print medium is increasingly giving way to the electronic form of materials. This study examines libraries by region within the State of Orissa, India. It examines the level of effort taken by the engineering college libraries in Orissa to build electronic resource.

HISTORICAL DEVELOPMENT OF DIGITAL LIBRARY

Although the term digital library has gained popularity in recent years; it has evolved along the technological ladder for past thirty years. In early 1970s, digital libraries were built around mini and main-frame computer providing remote access and online search and retrieval services to users using computer and communication technology available at the time and intended the release of a number of software packages for computer based storage, indexing and retrieval of documents in character coded form, e.g. STAIRS, IBM'S storage and information retrieval systems, BASIS (Battelle Automated Search Information Systems) etc. During 1980, sophisticated information storage and retrieval system came into light. On-line host like DILAOG and STN providing full text online journals, through simple ASCII or text files without graphic and pictures. In the late 1980's and early 1990's several full text databases started appearing i.e. IEE electronic library (IEL), (UMI'S international buyers database, US patent etc.1990 witnessed a revolution in digital library system with the introduction of World Wide Web, which offered a crucial advantage with the ability or ready to use and user friendly graphical web knowledge for all prevalent platforms. The Internet and associated technology made it possible for digital libraries to include multimedia objects like image, audio, video etc. The recent development in digital library can be attributed to international web technology. At that time the Gopher protocol was the primary cross platform protocol used to store, transmit and view information on the internet. Thereafter the Web replaced Gopher cross platform protocol used to store and view information on the internet.

WHAT IS DIGITAL LIBRARY

Digital library is a global virtual library is a library where information can be stored in electronic format containing texts, images, sound, video, maps, scientific and business data, as well as hypermedia combination of these elements. There will be vast population of user scattered around the globe, which are able to access, easily and conveniently.

ELECTRONIC RESOURCES

E-Resources are those resources which need computer access or any sort of electronic products that deliver a collection of data, it may be text referring to full text bases, electronic journals, image collections, other multimedia products and numerical, graphical or time bound. These may be delivered on CD-ROM on tape via Internet and so on. A number of techniques and related standard have been deployed which allow documents to be created and distributed in electronic form by over past years. In order to fulfill the users demand and provide better facilities, the library shifting towards new machine called Electronic Resource. The e-resource or magnate and optical media have a vast input on the collections of the libraries and these are more useful due to their inherit capabilities for manipulation and searching; provide information access in cheaper to acquiring information resources, saving in storage and maintenance, etc.

CATEGORIES OF E RESOURCE

E-resources have been divided into three different categories, Static, Dynamic and Living.**Static:** - The most basic that contains fixed information and it cannot be manipulated, i.e. online traditional data, Online Journals, E-Books, etc.**Dynamic:** - That contains fixed information but it can be manipulated their outward form, the way embedded material is presented to user i.e. Multi Media, CD-ROM, Diskettes, etc. **Living:** - That which can be manipulated both their form (outward appearance) and the sort of information is available in the Web.

STRATEGY FOR BUILDING E RESOURCE

A resource is any physical or virtual entity of limited availability, or anything used to help one earn a living. Digital Resources like E Book, E Journal E question e-thesis etc. The digital libraries provides two short of resources ie. (i) In-house resources and (ii) external resources

IN-HOUSE RESOURCES

In house resources are those resources that are stored in the web server locally and made accessible through the network. i.e C D ROM , Course materials and application notes E – question , post conference articles etc. It also knows as Institution Repository. Institution Repository plays a vital role to build in houses resources

INSTITUTION REPOSITORY

An institution repository is a tool for collection preserving and dissemination of the information into a Digital form. It is needed for higher education centers. It is an intellectual output for an institution. It is very useful for research Institute. It is a database in which a set of information are stored. It is useful to capture, index, preserve and redistribute an institute's scholarly research in digital forms and helpful for scholarly communication, storing learning materials and course ware, electronic publishing managing collections and preserving digital materials. Every institution has its own culture and assets that needs customized approach. One information model that best suits one institution may not suit for another institution.

OPEN SOFTWARE'S FOR INSTITUTIONAL REPOSITORIES

Software is the key element in the construction of an institutional repository. There are available two types of software: - subscribed and the free or open software.

Open software – An open software is the software, where the source code of the programs is made available for anyone to change and distribute provided they a abide the accompanying license. There is few most commonly available open software viz. **CDs Ware, Dspace, E-Prints, Fedora, i-Tor , Phronesis , MYCORE, ARNO,GSDL**

EXTERNAL RESOURCES

The external resources are those materials that are not stored in the web server, External resources includes online journals, online databases, e-book etc. External resources are provided by different publishers\ASME, ACM , IEEE, Oxford university Press Journal(OUP) and many more are there. The publisher provides access to their full text materials by two methods (i) username and password (ii) internet Protocol (IP) address based Access Control Method. E-Books E-Journals e- Databases

BUILDING EXTERNAL RESOURCE

External resource can be build through subscription of on line journal and online data-bases. There are number of different publishers of different subject in all over the world providing e-journal and e-databases service. Recently a new development in this area of the above service has evolved viz. Reference linking and pre-print service.

COST MINIMIZATION THROUGH BUILDING EXTERNAL RESOURCE

The explosion of information and inadequate library urged the libraries to adopt new philosophies and technologies for collection development and reduce the costs information. To achieve mutually the common objective a new concept has emerged is called E Journal Consortia. It is felt that the concept of E-Journals consortia can work well the libraries without requiring additional fees to access the e-journal

CONSORTIA

A Consortium could be described as a group of organizations who come together to fulfill a combined objective that usefully requires co-operation and the sharing of resources and need to have a clear mutual goal in order to ensure their success. The aim should be to deliver "more than the sum of the individual parts". A library Consortium formation can be local, regional, state, national and inter institutional level.

CONCLUSION

Engineering and Technology college libraries are facing challenges due to continuous reduction in the subscription to scholarly journals and databases which affect the research and academic activity. Many academic libraries have realized the importance of electronic sources of information in order to satisfy their end user, and among these E-journals have definitely had an impact on academic libraries. The professional journals that are available in the net have provided a great to the research and development work in the academic institutions, therefore the fast evolution and development of information and communication technology (ICT) has lead to more applications in recent years.

REFERENCE

1. Bajpai, R. P, Bidyut, K. Mal and Bajpai, G. "Use of e-resource through consortia: A Boon to users of Indian University Libraries" available at *crl.du.ac.in/ical09/papers/index_files/ical-85_83_195_2_RV.pdf.*
2. Choudhury, G G and Choudhury, Sudatta, Searching CD-ROM and online information source, London: Library association Publishing, 2001
3. Clifford A, Lynch and Joan K Lippincott " Insititutional Repository Deployent in the United States as of Early 2005 " D-Lib Magazine, September,2005, Vol-11, no-2
4. Devi, T. Madhuri, Vidyavati, Devi and Singh, I. "Available of E-resources and their access facility: a Case study of Manipur" available at am.inflibnet.ac.in:8080/dxml/handle/1944/1276.
5. Kannappanavar, B.U. and Vijayakumar, M. "Use of IT in University of Agricultural Science Libraries of Karnataka-A Comparative Study." DESIDOC Bulletin of Information Technology. Vol.21; 2001; 21-26p.
6. Kaur, Bajinder and Verma, R. " Use of Electronic information n Resources: A case study of Thaper University" available at publications.drdo.gov.in/ojs/index.php/djlit/article/view/243/153
7. Kumar, Aryun. "Use and Usage of electronic Resource in Business Schools in India: *FIIB" available at crl.du.ac.in/ical09/papers/index_files/ical-96_173_706_1_FB.pdf*
8. Mulla, K.R. "Information Technology: A Boon to E-learning." New Challenges in Information Management and E-learning in the Age of Globalization SIS 2003, IITCL, Roorkee; 2003; 134-141p.
9. Murthy, T.A.V, UGC-Infotech E-journals, INFLIBNET Newsletter,2006,3 (1)

10. Pandey, S K " Management of preserving e-sources in digital library in Indian Scenario : Chjhallenges and Prespectives " University News , 48 (07) 15-21, Feb, 2010.

11. Sahu, Mahendra and Mahapatra, R.K and Patra, N. "Electronic Resource in Academic Library: Usage Trends in Digital Environment " ICSSR National Seminar on " Dynamic of - resource and usage trends in digital era" during 10th & 11th sep, OUAT Camus, BBSR,2010,99-23-30

12. Webb, J.P. "Managing Licensed Networked Electronic Resources in a University Library". Information Technology Libraries. Vol.17; 1998; 198-206p.

23

Building E-Resources for Digital Libraries and the Changing World of Education

Salmon K

LIM Trainee, JRDTM Library, Indian Institute of Science, Bangalore-560012

Mansur K

LIM Trainee, IIM Library, Indian Institute of Management, Bangalore-560076

ABSTRACT

Libraries of all sizes and types are embracing digital collections, although most libraries will continue to offer both print and digital collections for many years to come. New purchase and purchases of journals, books, and magazines are heavily weighted toward digital, while digital books (e-books) are only beginning to become a presence in library collections. Libraries prefer digital collections for many reasons. The library can get usage statistics that are not available for print collections and digital collections save space and are relatively easy to maintain. When total processing and space costs are taken into account, electronic collections may also result in some overall reductions in library costs. We are on the threshold of a revolution that is making the world's accumulated information and knowledge accessible to individuals everywhere. Digital libraries aim to help in generating, sharing, and using knowledge so that communities become more efficient and productive and the benefits of collaboration are maximized. It seek Digital libraries are a set of electronic resources and associated technical capabilities for creating, searching, and using information; they are an extension and enhancement of information storage and retrieval systems that manipulate digital data in any medium.

Key words : Digital Library, E-resources, Electronic Journals and Electronic Resources.

INTRODUCTION

The term 'library' is defined by Encyclopedia Britannica Online as "traditionally, collection of books used for reading or study, or the building or room in which such a collection is kept". Technologies have made it possible to store and retrieve information in many different forms and from any place with a computer and a network connection. The term digital library and virtual library have begun to be used to refer to the vast collections of information to which people gain access over the internet, satellite television or some other type remote electronic connection". Libraries have always been valued for and measured by their collections. However, library budgets and space constraints have led many libraries to make choice of the formats for information resources they collect. The electronic publishing of books is increasing, e-journals are emerging and databases are costly yet provide lots of information for higher education especially in the field of science and technology. Electronic information is gaining more and more importance in the academic activities, especially in the field of engineering and technology with the drastic change in the pattern of dissemination of knowledge. The library is seen as a source of training and guidance to a community of learners who are concerned with navigating the complexities of locating and using digital resources and services. Moreover, the move towards a digital environment has resulted in a shift from the systematic one-to-one information ûow of the past to a new model in which the users and the providers of information are able to relate in a many-to-many, dynamic relationship They are, however, encouraged to trust in electronic resources with a presumption that, the wealth of information available in electronic formats can utterly accomplish their scholastic needs as a better substitute to traditional print services.

WHAT IS A DIGITAL LIBRARY?

- A DL is the combination of "content and services".
- A Digital Library is a "tool" at the centre of intellectual activity having no logical, conceptual, Physical, temporal, or personal borders or barriers on information.
- A DL is an "entity" providing the functionality to mediate between information objects and Information users in the context of distributed collections of information objects. This (External) functionality includes access, publish, delivery, preservation, personalization, etc.

DEFINING THE DIGITAL LIBRARY

1. "A digital library service is an assemblage of digital computing, storage, and communications machinery together with the software needed to reproduce, emulate, and extend the services provided by conventional libraries based on paper and other material means of collecting, storing, cataloguing, finding, and disseminating information." (Gladney H.M, et. al. 1994).
2. "Digital Libraries are a set of electronic resources and associated technical capabilities for creating, searching, and

using information...they are an extension and enhancements of information storage and retrieval systems that manipulate digital data in any medium (text, images, sounds,static or dynamic images) and exist in distributed networks" (Borgman, 1996).

HOW DIGITAL LIBRARIES WORK

- Digital libraries hold metadata records, and sometimes primary content. Have a defined scope of content, intended audience.
- Metadata describes the resource content, the intended user audience, resource type and other characteristics.
- Search over metadata and/or primary content to retrieve information about and links to relevant resources.

CHARACTERISTICS OF DIGITAL LIBRARY

1. Universal and unlimited access.
2. Contents will be in digital format which can be utilized only with the help of computer.
3. Contents in textual, image, sound and video form.
4. Collection to connection.

PURPOSE OF DIGITAL LIBRARY

- To develop information systems providing access to a coherent collection of materials, this will be in digital format and enable full utilization of the opportunities that are offered by the materials available in digital formats.
- Helps in the reduction of physical storage of information, consequentially lessons wear and tear of the materials.
- It enables several readers to view the same item at the same time on their respective desktops.
- Digital libraries prove to be more cost-effective.
- It supports library functions, such as circulation, serial control, acquisition work, stock maintenance and developing in-house database.

EXAMPLES OF DIGITAL LIBRARIES

- American Memory from the Library of Congress
  http://lcweb2.loc.gov/ammem/ammemhome.html
- University of California at Berkeley
  http://elib.cs.berkeley.edu/
- Internet Public Library
  http://www.ipl.org
- New York Public Library
  http://digital.nypl.org/

Digital Libraries: A Systems View

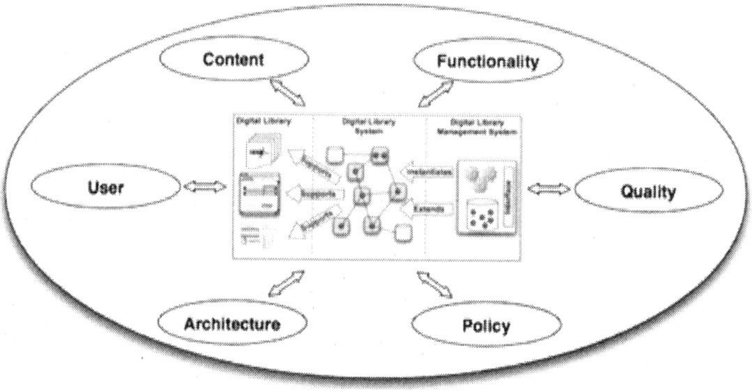

E-RESOURCES

In the words of Saye (2001), "electronic resources are the resources that are generated through some electronic medium and made available to a wide range of viewers both on-site and off-site via some electronic transferring machine or internet." Therefore, electronic resources in its ambit include all kinds of digital collections in the form of e-books, e-articles, e-databases, e-journals, electronic theses and dissertations (ETDs), e-standards and patents, e-reports, e-news, etc. Moreover, ICT has enabled the transformation of electronic information services in the forms of e-assignments, e-terms papers, e-project reports in many educational institutions and universities all across the world which impels the students' community to use electronic resources for the betterment of their academic needs. The author conceptualizes the following model that illustrates the transmission of e-resources in academic environment.

ELECTRONIC JOURNALS AND ELECTRONIC RESOURCES

Most library and information professional particularly in the third world lack ICT technical skills that are pertinent in e-resource environments. PC Troubleshooting for Library Personnel is a training programme that aims to enable each institution to develop a realistic PC troubleshooting diagnostic procedure appropriate to their circumstances. It seeks to impart skills to diagnose simple hardware, software, network and Internet problems in libraries and also enable the librarians to liase with the IT support department. E-resources management requires working knowledge of the Internet. It also requires technical skills to develop web pages so that the resources can be linked to library pages. The 'Web Page Design and Authoring, leading to Library Web Pages' training programme was designed to provide web design and authoring skills for library and information professionals and to highlight the importance of designing and building scalable, accessible and usable Web sites.

Benefits of nurturing your e-publication: Articles freely available online are more highly cited. For greater impact and faster scientific progress, authors and publishers should aim to make research easy to access.

LIFE CYCLE OF AN E-RESOURCE

Discovery – The awareness of new e-resources originates from a faculty members' request, a recommendation from a subject librarian. The librarian than locates information about the e-resources –information that might includes, for example the bibliographic details of an e-journal.

Trial – In many cases a librarian want to try out an e

resources before deciding whether to purchase a license for it. a trial enables the librarian the offer the e resources to some or all users. During the trial process, the librarian activates the e resource in the desire areas of the librarian environment, notifies the relevant and obtains feedback.

Selection – once the trial is over, the librarian decides whether to acquire the e resources.

Acquisition – If the librarian decides to go forward and subscribe to the resources, he or she carries out an Acquisition Process that somewhat resembles the process for print resources. Librarian acquiring e-journals as a part of a package from an e-resource aggregator.

Access – Access, of course is a major issue and you're dealing with e resources ones a library have acquired an e-resource, the librarian's wants to ensure that is well used.

Decision to renew or cancel – An e-resource subscription is typically valid for a defined time period. When the period ends, the librarian must either renew the subscription or cancel it. Whatever the outcome of the decision- renewal or cancelation- the system needs to support it. Provides access to the following full-text electronic journals and bibliographic databases to its academic fraternity for their research and development.

ROLE OF E-RESOURCES IN LIBRARIES

1. Exchange of information from internet to video conferencing
2. Simplified technology to create and distribute information with the help of library professionals.
3. Library as a center for learning resources.

E-resources include:

1. E-books.
2. CD-ROM/DVD Resources.
3. Online Resources.

4. Web-based resources.
5. E-journals
6. Databases.

FULL TEXT E-RESOURCES

1. American Chemical Society: www.pubs.acs.org
2. American Institute of Physics: http://scitation.aip.org/publications/
3. American Physical Society: http://scitation.aip.org/publications/myBrowsePub.
4. Annual Reviews: http://arjournals.annualreviews.org/
5. Wiley-Blackwell Publishing: www3.interscience.wiley.com/
6. Cambridge University Press: http://journals.cambridge.org/
7. Elsevier Science: www.sciencedirect.com/
8. Emerald: www.emeraldinsight.com
9. Institute of Physics: www.iop.org/EJ/
10. J-STOR: www.jstor.org/
11. Nature: www.nature.com/
12. Oxford University Press: www.oxfordjournals.org
13. Portland Press: www.portlandpress.com/pp/journals/default.htm
14. Project Euclid: http://projecteuclid.org/
15. Project Muse: http://muse.jhu.edu/
16. Royal Society of Chemistry: www.rsc.org/Publishing/Journals/
17. SIAM: http://epubs.siam.org/
18. Springer Link: www.springerlink.com/
19. Taylor and Francis: www.informaworld.com/

BIBLIOGRAPHIC DATABASES

1. SciFinder Scholar: www.cas.org/SCIFINDER/SCHOLAR/index.html
2. MathSciNet: www.ams.org/mathscinet/
3. Royal Society of Chemistry (6 Databases):
4. ISID: http://isid.org.in/
5. JCCC: http://jccc-ugcinfonet.in or www.jccc-ugcinfonet.in

OPEN ACCESS RESOURCES

1 About Open Access: www.oaeresources.html

2 Open Access E-Journals: www.oaeresources.html#ejournals

3 Open Access Directories: www.oaeresources.html#directories

4 IRs@member Institutions: www.oaeresources.html#IRs

TRENDS IN EDUCATION

- Wi-Fi™ access is expected – everywhere.
- Multiple Wi-Fi devices per student.
- Variety of devices, laptops, tablets, smart phones, games, etc.
- Connectivity everywhere – classrooms, lecture halls, dormitories, Cafeteria, library and campus.
- Faculty/Student applications.
- Lecture captures (video).
- Collaborative learning, Social networks.
- Skype, Pandora, Netflix, YouTube.
- Video surveillance, Wi-Fi phones

CONCLUSION

The concepts of Digital and Virtual libraries are actually services added to the traditional libraries wherein the resources which can only be utilized with computers. We hope digital libraries will consist with traditional libraries whether within them or as separate entities. However the role of professionals will be drastically changed in digital environment. Digital libraries have customers instead of users and provide pull and push information delivery methods. The internet is used as an efficient medium for accessing, collecting, storing, communicating and disseminating information worldwide. The result of this is that the use of internet is rapidly increasing in libraries to satisfy the needs of information seekers. The web is the largest treasure trove of information on the internet. It is the "World Bank of Information Sources, containing information on any branch of knowledge. The web provides worldwide access to various useful fee-based as well as free information sources. However, ûnancial barriers still handicap users from using fee-based information sources. Therefore, many institutions and organizations provide open access to their information sources. These sources and services can be accessed on the internet without paying any subscription charges to the publishers or authors. Users can access and download the required information available from these sources to their computers and can use it for academic and research purposes. The web contains a large number of open access sources such as books, journals, theses, dissertations, patents, standards, etc.

REFERENCE

1. E-resources: transforming access services for the digital age, Taryn Resnick., et al, library Hi tech, Vol 26 No1, 2008, 141-158pp.
2. Open access e-book collection on Central Asia in selected digital archives, Fayaz Ahmad
3. Loan, Collection Building 30/3 (2011) 126– 130pp Emerald Group Publishing Limited [ISSN 0160-4953]
4. Perception and usage of e-resources and the internet by Indian academics, B.T. Sampath Kumar, The Electronic Library Vol.28 No.1, 2010, 137-156pp
5. Students' keenness on use of e-resources Dillip K. Swain, The Electronic Library Vol. 28 No. 4, 2010 pp. 580-591.

6. E-Tools and the Globalised World of Learning and Communication, Juliet Stoltenkamp, Contemporary Educational Technology, 2010, 1(3), 208-220 208

24

Digital Library — An Overview

Ajay Khatri
Librarian, SRC Ayurved College, Chikhli
Dr. S.R. Baheti
Librarian, Smt. LRT College of Commerce, Akola,

ABSTRACT

Today we are the member of digital technology and that's why library personas are also competing to being all the users to library. Intact LIS professionals are successfully using all the computer technology in their daily routine work in short for automation and retrieval of information. But in this digital and 3G technology automation and computerization is not far sufficient for the libraries and so that we are adopting digital technology for impressing our users. Paper gives more information about digital library by focusing on its definition, characteristics, advantages, disadvantages and digital collection.

INTRODUCTION

We find that today readers are much more interested in digital libraries. Regarding these digital technology many large grant projects, an explosion of work performed by local individuals and institutions, international conferences, high activity in the computer science community, new journals dedicated to the subject, and a great deal of activity on the Internet. An Alta Vista search conducted in early July on "digital library" OR "digital libraries" retrieved about 20000 entries.

CHARACTERISTICS OF DIGITAL LIBRARIES

Digitized library require digital technologies and is the combination of traditional and media collection. So they encompass both paper and electronic material. Digital library consisted of mostly electronic documents, which are of reference type-

1. Digital Library is a digital object, which may be text, audio, video, image, and numeric multimedia components.
2. Digital library can be accessed from users work place.
3. Digital library support formal and informal learning procedures.
4. Digital library provides remote to rare and expensive material.

ADVANTAGES OF THE DIGITAL LIBRARY

The advantages of digital libraries as a means of easily and rapidly accessing books, archives and images of various types are now widely recognized by commercial interests and public bodies alike. Traditional libraries are limited by storage space; digital libraries have the potential to store much more information, simply because digital information requires very little physical space to contain it. As such, the cost of maintaining a digital library is much lower than that of a traditional library. A traditional library must spend large sums of money paying for staff, book maintenance, rent, and additional books. Digital libraries may reduce or, in some instances, do away with these fees. Both types of library require cataloguing input to allow users to locate and retrieve material. Digital libraries may be more willing to adopt innovations in technology providing users with improvements in electronic and audio book technology as well as presenting new forms of communication such as wikis and blogs; conventional libraries may consider that providing online access to their OPAC catalogue is sufficient. An important advantage to digital conversion is increased accessibility to users. They also increase availability to individuals who may not be traditional patrons of a library, due to geographic location or organizational affiliation.

- **No physical boundary** — The user of a digital library need not to go to the library physically; people from all over the world can gain access to the same information, as long as an Internet connection is available.
- **Round the clock availability** — A major advantage of digital libraries is that people can gain access 24/7 to the information.
- **Multiple access** — The same resources can be used simultaneously by a number of institutions and patrons. This may not be the case for copyrighted material: a library may have a license for "lending out" only one copy at a time; this is achieved with a system of digital rights management where a resource can become inaccessible after expiration of the lending period or after the lender chooses to make it inaccessible (equivalent to returning the resource).
- **Information retrieval** — The user is able to use any search term (word, phrase, title, name, subject) to search the entire collection. Digital libraries can provide very user-friendly interfaces, giving clickable access to its resources.
- **Preservation and conservation** — Digitization is not a long-term preservation solution for physical collections, but does succeed in providing access copies for materials that would otherwise fall to degradation from repeated use. Digitized collections and born-digital objects pose many preservation and conservation concerns that analog materials do not. Please see the following "Problems" section of this page for examples.

- **Space** — Whereas traditional libraries are limited by storage space, digital libraries have the potential to store much more information; simply because digital information requires very little physical space to contain them and media storage technologies are more affordable than ever before.
- **Added value** — Certain characteristics of objects, primarily the quality of images, may be improved. Digitization can enhance legibility and remove visible flaws such as stains and discoloration.

DISADVANTAGES OF DIGITAL LIBRARY

The computer viruses, lack of standardization for digitized information, quick degrading properties of digitized material, different display standard of digital product and its associated problem, health hazard nature of the radiation from monitor etc. makes digital libraries at times handicap.

1. **Copyright** — Digitization violates the copy right law as the thought content of one author can be freely transfer by other without his acknowledgement. So One difficulty to overcome for digital libraries is the way to distribute information. How does a digital library distribute information at will while protecting the copyright of the author?

2. **Speed of access** — As more and more computer are connected to the Internet its speed of access reasonably decreasing. If new technology will not evolve to solve the problem then in near future Internet will be full of error messages.

3. **Initial cost is high** — The infrastructure cost of digital library i.e. the cost of hardware, software; leasing communication circuit is generally very high.

4. **Band width** — Digital library will need high band for transfer of multimedia resources but the band width is decreasing day by day due to its over utilization.

5. **Efficiency** — With the much larger volume of digital information, finding the right material for a specific task becomes increasingly difficult.

6. **Environment** — Digital libraries cannot reproduce the environment of a traditional library. Many people also find reading printed material to be easier than reading material on a computer screen.

7. **Preservation** — Due to technological developments, a digital library can rapidly become out-of-date and its data may become inaccessible.

REQUIREMENT FOR DIGITAL LIBRARIES

The Internet and World Wide Web provide the impetus and technological environment for the development and operation of a digital library. The Internet provides the TCP/IP and or its associated protocol for accessing the information and web provide tools and technique for publishing the information over Internet. In the digital environment it is reasonable to say that a central back up or archive should be created at the national level, which will store information output of the region as well as information from outside the country. Some of the requirement for digital libraries is:

1. Audio visual: Color T.V., V.C.R., D.V.D., Sound box, Telephone etc.
2. Computer: Server, P.C. with multimedia, U.PS. Etc
3. Network: LAN, MAN, WAN, Internet etc.
4. Printer: Laser printer, Dot matrix, Barcode printer, Digital graphic printer etc
5. Scanner: H.P. Scan jet, flatbed, Sheet feeder, Drum scanner, Slide scanner, Microfilming scanner, Digital camera, Barcode scanner etc
6. Storage devices: Optical storage device, CD-ROM, Jukebox etc.
7. Software: Any suitable software, which is interconnected and suitable for LAN and WAN connection.

FACTORS OF CHANGE TO DIGITAL LIBRARIES

The limited buying power of libraries, complex nature of recent document, storage problem etc are some of the common factor which are influencing to change to digital mode, some other factors are-

1. Information explosion
2. Searching problem in traditional libraries
3. Low cost of technology: When we consider the storage capacity of digital document and its maintained then it can be easily realize that the cost of technologies is much more less than that of traditional libraries.
4. Environmental factor: the use of digital libraries is the cleanest technologies to fulfill the slogan "Burn a CD-ROM save a tree"
5. New generation needs.

ROLE OF LIBRARIAN IN DIGITAL ENVIRONMENT

Though the digital environment is built as a system, which can be used by its ultimate end user directly from their desktop pc, the role of librarian cannot be overlooked. In digital environment also the librarian and information scientist will be needed for packaging and repackaging of information, for electronic publishing, for reference purpose, to advise the user about the strategy to identify relevant electronic sources etc. thus the librarian will be more or less a hypertext engineer. In the new environment it will be very difficult for the librarian to decide what should be organized? How to give citation? How to organize the collection? Etc because the new environment will be really challenging one for the librarian to decide who are author who are publisher and who are user? . In the new environment anyone who has access to the network of digital libraries can be a publisher by merely posting messages to an online discussion group or by other means. A virtual environment is really open for all. In some cases, librarians have the opportunity to digitize unique material in their libraries' collections.

CHALLENGES FOR DIGITAL LIBRARIES

To achieve the broad vision of enabling access to any data (information, knowledge, answer, and digital object), digital libraries face many challenges, among them:

1. Searching for text, images, sound, and composite objects – multimedia search.
2. Semantically enhanced search to improve retrieval from free text and image content and to better exploit user-assigned tags.
3. Search across many languages multilingual search.
4. Search across many systems {syntactic and semantic interoperability.
5. Finding answers, not just documents; reasoning and inference.

CONCLUSION

Digital libraries are not going to replace the physical existence of document completely but no doubt to meet the present demand, to satisfy the non local user digitization must be introduced so that at least libraries becomes of hybrid nature. The initial cost of digitization is high but experiment shows that once digitization is introduced then the cost to manage this collection will be cheaper than that of any traditional library. Day by day the cost of digitization is decreasing, the online publication is increasing, the needs of user are shifting towards a different environment so it's needless to say that after one or two years my library or your library will go to be digitized so it's the pick time to all informational and library professional that they geared themselves to take the challenge. The success of the design, development and evaluation of digital libraries depends on the study of user and organization needs.

REFERENCES

1. Arms, William Y. (1995). Key Concepts in the architecture of the digital library. D-Lib magazine. 1-5
2. Borgman, C. (2000). Gutenberg to the Global Information Infrastructure: Access to Information in the Networked World. MIT Press, Cambridge.
3. Budhu M. and Coleman A. (2002). The Design and Evaluation of interactivities in a Digital Library. D-Lib Magazine. 8(11). 1-19.
4. en.wikipedia.org/wiki/Institutional_repository (accessed on 10/09/2008)
5. Ghosh, S. B., Open access and Institutional Repository a developing country perspective: A Case Study of India, 72nd IFLA General Conference 20-24 Aug 2006
6. Gladney H. M. (1994). Digital Library: Gross Structure and Requirement. http://www.csdl.tamu.edu/DL94/paper/fox.html
7. Hirwade, Mangala and Hirwade, Anil Institutional Repositories : Challenges and opportunity for LIS professional in Digital Age
8. http://dublincore.org/documents/2002/04/14/dcq-rdf-xml/images/hedgehog.gif
9. http://www.loc.gov/standards/premis/ICDAT2006/images/Slide15_gif.jpg
10. Jain P. K. (2007). LIS Education in India: Challenges for Students and Professionals in the Digital Age. LISU. 481-488
11. Kahle, B. (1997). Preserving the Internet. www.sciam.com/0397issue/0397kahle.html.
12. Kalam A. P. J. Abdul (2007). Indomitable Sprit. Rajpal & Sons, Delhi. 177-179.
13. Kenney, A. and Rieger, O. (2000). Moving Theory into Practice: Digital Imaging for Libraries and Archives. Research Libraries Group, Mountain View, CA, 2000.
14. Lesk, M. (1997). Practical Digital Libraries: Books, Bytes, and Bucks. Morgan Kaufman Publishers, San Francisco.
15. Levy, D. M., & Marshall, C. C. (1995). Going digital: a look at the assumptions underlying digital libraries. Communications of the ACM, 38(4), 77±84.
16. Lucier, R. E. (1995). Building a digital library for the health sciences: information space complementing information place. Bulletin of the Medical Library Association, 83(3), 346±350.
17. Lyman, P. (1996). What is a digital library? Technology, intellectual property, and the public interest. In Books, bricks, and bytes. Daedalus,

Journal of the American Academy of Arts and Sciences; Proceedings of the American

18. Malviya Rama Nand (2008). Digital Library and Academic Society in India. Asian Books, New Delhi. 3-25.

19. National Information Standards Organization. The Dublin Core Metadata Element Set: Draft Standard Z39.85; see www.niso.org/Z3985.html.

20. Oppenheim C. and Smithson D. (1999). What is the Hybrid Library? Journal of Information Science. 25(2). 97-112.

21. Rao, P. Venkata, Institutional Repositories: A Key Role For Libraries, International CALIBER 2007-Panjab University, Chandighar. pp 689-695

22. Robinson, Mary, Institutional Repositories: Staff and Skills requirements,8th August 2007 university of Nottingham, http://www.sherpa.ac.uk/documents/sherpaplusdocs/nottsRepository%20Staff%20and%20Skills.pdf (accessed on 10/09/2008)

23. Singh, S. N. and other, Open Source Software: A comparative Study of Greenstone and Dspace , International CALIBER 2007-Panjab University, Chandighar. Pp 89-97

24. Vishala, B.K., and Bhandi, M.K., Building Institutional Repository (IR):Role of the Library, International CALIBER 2007-Panjab University, Chandighar. pp 631-640

25. Zhao, D. G., & Ramsden, A. (1995). Report on the ELINOR electronic library pilot. Information Services and Use, 15, 199-212.

25

Transformation of B. N. College of Engineering, Pusad Library: Traditional to Digital

Dr. Prashant P. Deshmukh

Ex. Librarian, B.N. College of Engineering, Pusad-445 215, Dist. Yavatmal (MS)

ABSTRACT

This article describes transformation of Babasaheb Naik College of Engineering; Pusad Library, that has brought about significant change by providing integrated information services to the campus community. Information and Communication Technology has revolutionized the concept of libraries. Each and every library is slowly getting digitized and Digital environment is open for all. This paper will discuss the factors which will necessitate the traditional libraries to get digitized. The authors describe the change process (phase wise and step wise), initiatives towards digital library, new approach of transformation as well as the obstacles encountered and the strategies employed to overcome them.

Keywords : Digital Library, Information Communication Technology, Transformation of Library

INTRODUCTION

Technology has impacted libraries significantly, whether it is decreased door counts or increased use of virtual resources and especially academic libraries have faced a great deal of change in recent years. Users have more options than ever for filling their information needs. LIS Professionals must be creative and innovative in order to serve their users to the fullest. Professionals have to reach more users in a variety of ways, as their collections and services move into an increasingly virtual environment, they have to provide their users greater access to in-house as well external resources which is exactly what they want.

Now information personnel's have to work harder than ever before to get out into their users spaces (both physically and virtually) and to draw their users into the traditional space of the library. What follows is an overview of the initiatives and strategies in Engineering Library have implemented to reach out to

ABOUT LIBRARY

BNCOE Pusad library with a rich collection of engineering, science and technology books, periodicals etc. catering to the academic and research needs of teachers, research scholars & postgraduate and undergraduate students. The libraries which collectively support the teaching, research and extension programmes of the Institute. All students, faculty members and employees of the Institute are entitled to make use of the Library facilities on taking library membership. The Library, besides having a huge collection of books on engineering, science and humanities offers library services through its various divisions. Library has more than 2000 active members.

RE-ENGINEERING WITH THE USE OF NEW APPROACH AND NETWORKING TECHNOLOGY

The technological revolutions have become order of the days. There is a revolution brewing in the world of information, communications and technology, and for a change, the telecom companies or the Internet Service Providers is not driving it. Fast changing curricula and frequent introduction of new subjects impose a great demand on the system in general. Technology is a driving force in the contemporary education systems. Successful implementation of high-tech programmers like INDEST consortia resources will really get further strengthened and campus wide reach with the adoption of cabled network and wireless technologies.

APPLICATION OF LEASE LINE AND WI-FI

A separate LAN was installed inside the BNCE library. Initially 28 machines were installed. At present all machines have been connected via the library LAN. The library LAN in turn is connected to the institute Intranet, thus providing accessibility of library resources to all parts of the campus including students hostels, faculty wing and faculty residential areas. Library has been subscribing 2 mbps internet connectivity for fast and better access of E-resources. All the 28 terminals have been connected by cat 5 cables through the various switches installed on different location in the library and along with that parallel wi-fi connectivity has also been provided for reliable and smooth access. The Wi-Fi technology have been adopted due to the faster and cheaper net connection; allows for a more dynamic network, free network without cables; spread out at a larger table in a quieter area of the campus; flexibility which allows to move about without breaking the network connection. It is available to users both when the library is open, and when it is closed. It can be achieved either by the user's own wireless-enabled device or by a wireless device provided to them by the college. This could be a laptop with a connection outside of the library would only be possible within

100-300 meters of the building and further it can be extended with the use of additional antennas and access points.

With the re-engineering of new approach and networking technology, in-house activities and services of library could be extended to the user community at their desktops without much physical environ rather wireless at a higher speed than now to justify the realization of five laws of library science laid down by Dr S R Ranganathan. Thus, the user's time consciousness approach for want of information can be met out of networking through Wi-Fi feasible technology, where bandwidth and physical layout would be at its advantage.

INITIATIVES TOWARDS TRANSFORMATION TO LIBRARY AUTOMATION

Even after having a huge shortage of staff in library, we have planned re-engineering of library automation, about 60,000 books database had been managed in LibSYS Software.

First Phase

Initial necessary hardware such as server, scanners, computer systems, CD-writer, 5 in one printers, Bar-code reader its printer and internet and intranet tools were procured.

Second phase

Readymade library management software named LibSYS was procured and installed and further project for retrospective conversion were initiated step by step....

Step-1 : Data from CDS / ISIS ...The data of books available in CDS/ISIS have been imported into LibSYS.

Step-2 : Database for holdings and members.....Without wasting time we decided to first enter all the record through the accession register by entering all the information available in the accession register. Due to the availability of limited number of library staff, the work was executed on contract basis through an outside agency. But the database for the members was created by the staff.

Step-3 : Entry of class number..... The library accession register does not contain class numbers. The class numbers in the computer were updated.

Step -4 : OPAC.....OPAC was a first computerized activity provided to the library users.

Step -5 : LibSYS training for library staff ..... An informal training programme on the use of LibSYS was organized for the staff at B.N. College of Engineeing, Pusad Library

Step -6 : Automated Circulation.... After having the clear concept on the circulation activities of LIBSYS, computerized issue / return of books had been carried out simultaneously with the manual for six months and after that it was shifted completely on automated system.

Step-7 : Editing and key wording through books....The library databases is being edited and due key words is also being assigned. During this period, all the bibliographical records of books are also being updated.

Step-8 : Preparation of Bar-coded library membership card....Bar-coded membership card was introduced and implemented for library facilities including circulation.

Step-9 : Bar-code label printing and pasting .....Library procured the barcode printer and allied stationary. Two barcode labels for each document was got printed and pasted (one on front page and another below the due date slip page) by the library staff.

INITIATIVE TOWARDS TRANSFORMATION TO DIGITAL LIBRARY

With the advent of Information Technology revolution the role of Information Systems and the Libraries are undergoing a rapid change and it is important for us to understand and exploit as to how best we can assimilate the impact on Information Technology for the rapid track development of modern techniques driven Information Systems and the Libraries. Along with the automation of library services, we would like to move one step towards the digitalization of library resources.

To make the B.N.College of Engineering Library a 21st Century Knowledge Centre to facilitate the transition of today's engineering society to a knowledge base society of tomorrow. It is necessary that the knowledge generated by the faculty and students of BNCOE is digitized and made accessible through Intranet or Internet. The practice of digitalization of resources will be a continuing process in the library and all students, research scholars and faculty members are contributing their publications.

Procurement of Electronic Resources and CD Storage Systems

Digital library activities were initiated with the procurement of some index databases such as. Library has been the member of INDEST Consortia for last four year. Being an AICTE supported institution the facility of online journals like IEEE/IEE, ASME, ASCE, etc. are extended to us. For effective and efficient management of CD-ROMs, a CD Storage system is being under process at BNCOE library.

Formation of INDEST User Group

To maximize the utilization of online journals, and speeding up the awareness among students and faculty members, INDEST Users Group (IUG) of voluntary students and faculty members in the college under the Chairman of Library Advisory Committee have been set up and all interested students and faculty members have joined the IUG.

User Education

The INDEST Users Group is responsible to organize awareness meets on regular intervals. During the meet, the following activities are carried out.

- Training programme for effective use of available online journals.
- Lectures by experts of other institutions using INDEST facilities.

- Group discussion on problems faced by users.

At the beginning of each academic session, library organize orientation programme through the live demonstration of College website to educate the new users about the library resources and methods for using the services. Besides that 28 computers have been installed in the library for the use of students. On these computers, students can access the library services: check their accounts, library OPAC, putting of reservations, on-line search (Internet, E-journals), Use of CD Diskettes available in the library, and view all other library services.

Services to the Users

Services to the users are major function of any library and users are expected to visit Library services more frequently. Under this module, further links to the following services has been provided.

Registration

The link to down load the registration form has been provided and all the faculty member and newly admitted students of the college have to register them self before enjoying the library facility. Other terms for registration along with complete rule and regulation of the library have been provided so that users may go through before registration. Users may registered them self online, however they have to collect their laminated library ID from the library personally.

Cancellation of Registration / No Dues Certificate

Schedule for No Dues Certificate have been provided online along with the form, which may be downloaded from the library services.

Reference Service

A large number of Encyclopedias, Handbooks are available in the Library Reference staff is also available in the reading room to suggest sources of information and to assist in locating the required material and link is also provided for online reference queries.

Newspaper and Magazine Section

List of all 18 national newspapers and 60 magazines which are being subscribed in the library have been placed.

Journals/Periodicals Section

Journals being the primary source of information are essential to supplement the research activities and are required regularly. A number of foreign & Indian journals are being subscribed Full Text on-line to facilitate the on going research activities & to expand the areas of future research activities. The online Journals being subscribed include ASME, ASCE, IEL (IEE/IEEE). The users can access of e-journals from anywhere at any time because these Login id and Password based.

Library Catalogue (OPAC)

The library offers computerized catalogue search services through the OPAC. The bibliographic record consisting of more than 60,000 books available in the Central Library. Sufficient numbers of PCs are placed in the user area for the students and faculty to access the OPAC. Our Library Catalogue can also be searched through Internet.

Recommend a Book

Members may recommend any document to procure in the library, a requisition form for the purpose is available in the library Services Link. They may submit the form online by providing document details along with their personal details. As and when he request received in the library mail, after checking the holding, same is forwarded to chairman, LAC financial approval. Purchase for the book processed after online approval and on paper approval processed later on in the file. This facility is also available through LibSYS OPAC also. Members however may recommend any document by using printed form which is available in the library.

Book Bank

The College runs a Book Bank intended to assist students, from the economically weaker sections of society, by giving text books on loan to deserving students for a hole academic semester according to the rules framed for the purpose.

Special Collection for SC/ST category

Selected text books are made available to issue for a period of one semester according to the rules framed for this purpose to the student belonging to SC/ST category. Eligible students may apply for books from the special collection as per the schedule announced by the library.

Xerox / Printing Service

Based on requisition, Xerox copies of the library documents are made available mainly for academic purpose.

Library OPAC and Recent Additions

Library has installed library software named LibSYS for managing the library affairs for providing bibliographical information of the library holdings and other additional facility to the users. Through the Intranet, access of library resources has been extended to the user's desk. Apart from the OPAC, a list of books with bibliographic records has also been displayed annually or monthly which has been added in the library collection.

Introducing Online Requisition

To inculcate the participation and to know user need to build up the library collection, online request form for procurement of any document is provided, users may submit their request to library, the details in this regards can viewed under section 6.1.11 recommend a book.

LAC: - (Library Advisory Committee)

In this menu there is a list of the library representatives from various departments and chairman of library advisory committee. Users can know the names and designations of their library representative and chairman of LAC. In respect of library affairs any user may contact to their respective library representatives.

Computerization and Digitization

The information regarding computerization and digitization going on in the library has been provided. To provide good library services with save the time of user and staff too we are doing computerization of library services. We are using LibSYS software package which is an integrated multi user library system. Now many of the work of the library like issue/return (circulation), acquisition work, and OPAC etc. are done by this software library management software.

CONCLUSION

There are many ways to engage our users through new technologies, orientation activities, and invite them to use the library services. We tried our best to satisfy the needs of our users. But we are still waiting for the maximum utilization of the library services through Intranet. A few new advance features have been introduced and the users need to train how to utilize them for the maximum result. In the BNCOE, we continue to explore new ways to connect with both traditional library users and new users who have never visited the library. By viewing changes in technology and communication patterns as opportunities to reach our users rather than as barriers that keep them away, we are better able to serve our community.

REFERENCES

1. Breeding, M. (2002). "A hard look at wireless networks". Library-Journal, Net Connect Supplement Summer: 14-17
2 Glaskin, M. (2002). "Live and unplugged".*New*-Scientist, 176 (2365), p.38-9.
3 Sharma, P.B. (November 13, 2000) " Libraries and Information Systems in the New Millennium, Keynote Address at XIX IASLIC National Seminar, Bhopal

4 Mundell, Carrick. 2005. *Amazon - Seattle Public Library Lookup Greasemonkey Script Updated.* [Online]. Available: http:// www.mundell.org/2005/12/08/amazon-seattle-public-library-lookup-greasemonkey -script-updated/ [January 13, 2006]

5 J. Darcy Duke, Stephanie Hartman and Angela Locknar: "Reaching the Engineering and Science Communities: New Technologies and Approaches at MIT", Science and Technology Librarianship, Winter 2006

6 Udell, John. 2005. *The Library Lookup Project.* [Online]. Available: http:/ /weblog.info world.com/udell/stories/2002/12/11/librarylookup.html [January 13, 2006].

7 Gaur, Ramesh C. "Reengineering Library and Information Services: Process People and Technology". Allied Publishers, Mumbai, 2003

8 Morris, D E, Resarcak, P and Rowley, G Monographic acquisitions : staffing costs and the impact of automation Library resources and technical services 40(4) 1996 p307

9 White, H. (1993). Scholarly publication, academic libraries, and the assumption that these processes are really under management control. *College k Research Libraries,* 54(4), 293-301

26

Applications of Cloud Computing in Libraries and Information Centers

Sheetal D Naik

Librarian, College of SVIMS Pune

Nandkumar B Dahibhate

Principal Technical Officer, National Chemical Laboratory Pune

ABSTRACT

Information and communication technology is used extensively in libraries and information centers due to its multifold benefits and new avenues are up coming in the area of LIC. The libraries have been automated, networked and now moving towards paper less or virtual libraries. To meet the challenges in the profession librarians are also applying different platforms in LIC's for attaining economy in information handling. This paper overviews the basic concept of newly developing area known as cloud computing. The use of cloud computing in libraries and how cloud computing actually works is illustrated in this communication.

Key words: Cloud Computing, Cloud computing and libraries

INTRODUCTION

Libraries and Information Centers are facing many challenges in the profession due to applications of ICT (Information & Communication Technology). New concepts are being added to ease the practices in the society, and libraries and information centers are also accepting many new technologies in the profession as they suit the present information handling and they satisfy needs of the knowledge society. With the advent of ICT, libraries have become automated which is the basic need towards advancement followed by networks and more efforts are towards virtual libraries. This is necessary to provide information to the users instantly and economically. The emergence of e-publications, digital libraries, Internet usage, Web tools applications for libraries, consortium practices leads to the further developments in LIS (Library & Information Science) profession. The latest technology trend in LIC (Library & Information Center) is use of cloud computing for various purposes and for achieving economy in library functions. Since cloud computing is a new and core area, the professionals should be aware of it and also the applications of Cloud computing in LIS.

CLOUD COMPUTING

Cloud computing is the technology of computing, which is totally based on internet media. Using internet technology many servers share resources in terms of offering common platform for use of software applications, different resources including information, networking computer and devices which are attached on request with the control of electricity grid. It can also be called as the service architecture or virtualization for improving the utility of the computational techniques. Complete cloud computing system is service oriented and customer focused. The main concept behind cloud computing is based on the cloud that is specifically designed for the processing each related device located in cloud of network. Could computing remains invisible to the customer's or users (http://www.wifinotes.com/computer-networks). The users or the service provider using cloud needs to pay for their resources and services rendered used in cloud computing environment.

DEFINITIONS

In the Internet environment web tools are more useful and applied for scholarly and scientific communication. Few concepts associated with cloud computing are:

CLOUD COMPUTING

Since the term is new it is necessary to review it in different angles to apply it appropriately. Many definitions for cloud computing are expressed by the technologist among which most basic concept dragged out is "cloud computing is the availability of ICT based needs offered as services, often through a third party vendor acting as a commercial mediator for facilitating the shared services to the enterprises.

Finally the term Cloud Computing means –

- Customers do not own network resources, like hardware, software, systems etc;
- Network resources are provided through remote data centers on a commercial and subscription basis; and
- Network resources are delivered as service over the web.

It has many advantages and recently proved as a resource sharing faculty in the information society.

CLOUD NETWORKING

Cloud networking is one of the networking based technology or technique that is responsible for facilitating the computer networks with the required resources. Cloud networking provides the resource when computer networks ask for the resource. They work exactly in the same way as other service providers company such as gas supply, telephone, electricity and gas supply companies. The list of the resources provided by the cloud networking to its users is in the simplest form so that its readers can understand them easily. The service providers facilitating its users with the abstract internet services is known as cloud.

ADVANTAGES OF THE CLOUD COMPUTING

- Cloud computing enables user to frequently use the technological resource at inexpensive price.
- It is accessible and reliable interface for its users API technology make it more interesting for the users to interact with the human beings.
- These computing techniques greatly reduce the total cost and capital expenses that come in arranging the infrastructure. Integrated resources are available at almost no cost to the third party users.
- Cloud computing is completely geographically independent. Its users can access the system from the web browsers anywhere in the world at any time.
- Multi and Large application pool is available for the users.
- **Reliability** improved design versions of many redundant website have efficiently increase the performance and suitability of cloud computing more useful.
- Security: Security is at one level above as compared to the other networks because of the centralization of data and increased security feature of every individual component.
- Cloud computing systems are flexible and easy to maintain because components can be added and deleted from the infrastructure.

WHAT IS CLOUD COMPUTING?

According to Wikipedia (http://en.wikipedia.org/wiki/Cloud_computing) cloud computing is the delivery of computing as a service rather than a product, whereby shared resources, software and information are provided to computers and other devices as a utility (like the electricity grid) over a network (typically the Internet).

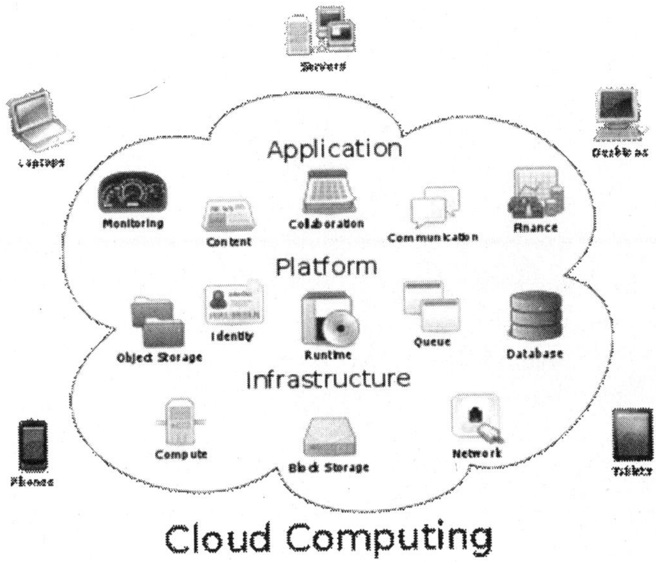

Source: http://en.wikipedia.org/wiki/Cloud_computing

Cloud computing provides computation, software, data access, and storage services that do not require end-user knowledge of the physical location and configuration of the system that delivers the services. Parallels to this concept can be drawn with the electricity grid, wherein end-users consume power without needing to understand the component devices or infrastructure required to provide the service.

The concept of cloud computing fills a perpetual need of IT: a way to increase capacity or add capabilities on the fly without investing in new infrastructure, training new personnel, or licensing new software. Cloud computing encompasses any subscription-based or pay-per-use service that, in real time over the Internet, extends IT's existing capabilities.

Knorr and Gruman (http://www.infoworld.com/d/cloud-computing/what-cloud-computing-really-means-031) describes cloud computing as a new supplement, consumption, and delivery model for ICT services based on Internet protocols, and it typically involves provisioning of dynamically scalable and often virtualized resources. It is a byproduct and consequence of the ease-of-access to remote computing sites provided by the Internet. This may take the form of web-based tools or applications that users can access and use through a web browser as if they were programs installed locally on their own computers (The Economist).

Cloud computing providers deliver applications via the internet, which are accessed from a Web browser, while the business software and data are stored on servers at a remote location. In some cases, legacy applications (line of business applications that until now have been prevalent in thin client Windows computing) are delivered via a screen-sharing technology, while the computing resources are consolidated at a remote data center location; in other cases, entire business applications have been coded using web-based technologies such as AJAX.

Most cloud computing infrastructures consist of services delivered through shared data-centers and appearing as a single point of access for consumers' computing needs. Commercial offerings may be required to meet service level agreements (SLAs), but specific terms are less often negotiated by smaller companies (Buyya et al)

CHARACTERISTICS OF CLOUD COMPUTING

Gens (2008) while defining cloud computing and cloud services pointed out some characteristics of cloud computing which states: agility, application program interface, cost, device, reliability, scalability, performance, security, maintenance and sustainability etc. These characteristics are useful for the service provision through cloud.

CLOUD COMPUTING MODELS

The different models are public cloud, community cloud, hybrid cloud, private cloud, and intercloud etc. These models are representing different utility models. But in all the models of Cloud computing technology used is the internet and central remote servers to maintain data and applications. Cloud computing allows consumers and businesses to use applications without installation and access their personal files at any computer with internet access. This technology allows for much more efficient computing by centralizing storage, memory, processing and bandwidth.

HOW CLOUD COMPUTING ACTUALLY WORKS?

Cloud computing involves the multiple cloud components that communicate with each other with the help of application interfaces mostly web services. UNIX operating system follows the same theoretical techniques for its tasks. The task complexity is divided into all the components making balanced and manageable results. The two most important components are the back end and front end. The front end is the interface or the main screen that is visible to the customers and users through which they interact with the system. This interface can be browsed with the help of web browsers and all the applications can be used with this interface. Usually this interface is GUI based. The back end involves all the components and the complete architecture and programming technique of cloud computing that totally remains hidden from the users. Only the system knows what is going on at the backend for every user request. The back end devices involve, cloud server, assistant computers, Data storage media and many connectors.

Cloud computing involves a diffuse, distributed computing infrastructure provided through the internet in an abstract way where programmers and users of the service need to be involved with the specific supporting hardware components. This model offers both data storage and computer processing capabilities. Programmers that develop cloud based applications make calls to servers that involve computational processing or data storage based on an application programming interface that addresses resources provided by a cloud provider.

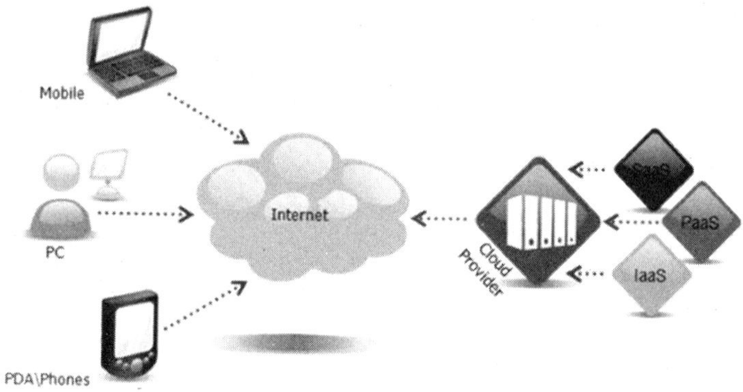

One of the well known providers of cloud services is Amazon.com with its Elastic Computed Cloud (EC2) service for computational transactions and Simple Storage Service (S3) for cloud based data storage. Google offers its App engine as a platform for cloud based services. Dozens of other companies offer public, private, or hybrid cloud services, each with different characteristics and benefits. Once a library is ready to deploy applications of cloud, it will be able to select from multitude of providers.

The Cloud or Cloud Computing refers to the use of internet services to provide applications, storage, and processing power to smaller web connecting computing devices. Small drives in notebook PC can use the cloud for extended storage, and portable devices like the iPhone or the new Google powered Android phones can be connected to applications on the cloud to duplicate desktop functionalities. In many cases cloud computing is for small public libraries, though school libraries may face additional challenges in coordinating with technology departments.

CLOUD COMPUTING IN LIBRARIES AND INFORMATION CENTERS

Cloud computing offers many interesting possibilities for libraries that may help to reduce technology costs and increase capacity reliability, and performance for some type of automation activities. Cloud computing has made strong inroads into other commercial sectors and is now beginning to find more applications in LIC.

The cloud computing pushes hardware to more abstract levels. Most of us are acquainted with fast computing power being delivered from systems that we can see and touch.

ROLE OF CLOUD COMPUTING IN LIBRARIES

Cloud computing is a completely new ICT based technology and it is known as 3rd Revolution after PC and Internet. Cloud computing is an enhancement of distributed computing, parallel computing, grid computing and distributed databases (Xiaona 2010). Among these, grid and utility computing are known as predecessors of cloud computing. Cloud computing has large potential for libraries. Libraries may put more and more content into the cloud. Using cloud computing user would be able to browse a physical shelf of books, CDs, or DVDs or choose to take out an item or scan a bar code into his mobile device. All historical and rare documents would be scanned into a comprehensive, easily searchable database and would be accessible to any researcher. Many libraries already have online catalogues and share bibliographic data with OCLC. More frequent online catalogues are linked to consortium that share resources.

Data storage could be a main function of libraries, particularly those with digital collections. Storing large digital files can stress local server infrastructures. The files need to be backed up, maintained, and reproduced for patrons. This can strain the data integrity as well as hog bandwidth.

Moving data to the cloud may be a leap of faith for some library professionals. It's a newer technology, and on the surface it is believed that libraries would have some control over this data or collections. However, with faster retrieval times for patron's requests and more local server space, it could improve storage solutions for libraries. Cloud computing or IT infrastructure that exists remotely, often gives users increased capacity and less need for updates and maintenance, and has gained wider acceptance among librarians.

ADVANTAGES OF CLOUD COMPUTING IN LIBRARIES

Cost Saving

In an era of shrinking budgets, it gets harder with each passing year to justify the purchase and maintenance of servers that aren't in use almost all the time. Cloud computing offers price savings due to economies of scale and the fact that you're only paying for the resources you actually use.

Flexibility and innovation

Libraries can take more risks when it comes to creative, innovative technology ideas when the new application will run on someone else's infrastructure. Libraries don't have to decide between devoting their limited server resources to the OPAC's overflow traffic and a new mobile web application that one of your colleagues wants to develop. If they're both hosted in the cloud, the resources devoted to each will shrink and expand as traffic rises and drops. Furthermore, creating and configuring new virtual server instances is fast and easy in the cloud.

Broad, general IT skills vs. deep, specialized skills

Cloud computing increases the pressure on IT professionals to become well-rounded employees with highly-developed managerial skills. Knowing how to configure and network a server isn't enough. Systems librarians have to manage complex projects and evaluate competing vendors on a variety of criteria. Holding vendors accountable is especially important when they manage a significant chunk of your online data and IT infrastructure.

Therefore, as long as cloud security remains a significant concern, techies may be called upon to help write binding, enforceable contracts that hold vendors to certain standards with regards to reliability and security of their services. Furthermore, techies will likely be part of the teams that periodically audit cloud vendors and ensure they're performing up to the contracted standards.

Additionally, there are few more advantages as follows:

- User centric
- Openness
- Transparency
- Interoperability
- Representation
- Availability anytime anywhere
- Connect and converse
- Create and collaborate

CLOUD COMPUTING SERVICES

- Serial solutions
- Delivering customized services
- Open infrastructure (e.g. Amazon, EC2, MS Azure)
- Publishing (e.g. Wordpress.com, twitter, YouTube)
- File Storage (e.g. Flickr, Dropbox, Jungle Disk, Google docs)
- Social Networking (e.g. Facebook, flickr, foursquare, LinkedIn)
- Integrated library systems
- Enterprise search
- Digital asset management
- Electronic resource management systems
- Web-based management systems
- OCLC based ILS services
- Circulation, acquisition, cataloguing, search

- Cloud-based services, data collaboration (e.g. Lockss)
- Service catalogue (SaaS, PaaS, LaaS)

Cloud computing is a phrase used today to describe the act of storing, accessing & sharing data, applications and computing power in cyber space (internet environment). The outcome of cloud computing is development of new computing models for end users.

EXAMPLES OF LIBRARIES IN THE NETWORK/CLOUD

- OCLC
- Library of Congress (LC)
- Exlibris
- POLARIS
- Scribd
- Discovery service
- Google Docs/ Google Scholar
- Worldcat
- Encore

CONCLUSION

Cloud computing is the next big wave in computing. It stands to change Information Technology services for many environments. It has many benefits, one of which is betterment of hardware management, since all the computers are the same and run the same hardware. It also provides better and easier management of data security, since all the data is located on a central server. Today cloud computing is the beginning of 'network based computing' over internet in force. It is the technology of the decade. There are innumerable benefits of cloud computing in library and other organizations. Libraries in the future may have the objectives to transfer manual effort into valuable activity. For this purpose, use of web as primary technology would be a better option and professionals should be trained for the same.

REFERENCES

- Buyya, R and others. Market oriented cloud computing. Accessed at http://www.cloudbus.org/~raj/papers/hpcc2008_keynote_cloudcomputing.pdf, accessed on 25-8-11
- Knorr, E and Gruman, G. What cloud computing really means. Accessed at http://www.infoworld.com/d/cloud-computing/what-cloud-computing-really-means-031, accessed on 25-8-2011)
- The Economist. Cloud computing. Clash of the clouds. Accessed at http://www.economist.com/node/14637206?story_id-14637206, accessed on 25-8-11
- Xiaona, F. and Lingyun, B. (2010) Application of Cloud Computing in University Library User Service Model. 2010 3rd international conference on advanced computer theory and engineering (ICACTE) V3 (144-147)

27

Using RFID Tags with Security Mechanism in Library Management

B.V. Chalukya

Librarian, Shri Chhatrapati Shivaji College, Omerga, Dist. Osmanabad (M.S.)

D.E. Dadpe

Librarian, Lokmanya Tilak Mahavidlaya, Wadawani, Dist. Beed (M.S.)

ABSTRACT

This paper presents a methodology of using low cost RFID tags for a library management system to protect the books from unauthorized capturing and usage. Every object to be identified in the RFID system is physically labeled with a tag. In the proposed method a book or a magazine or a CD is identified with the RFID tag. Whenever a book is issued to any user of the library, the RFID reader will capture the information of that book and compares it with the related information of the book in the Online Public Access Catalogue (OPAC) and issues the book to the user depending on his identity in the database. If any unauthorized person intends to take the book the RFID reader will immediately respond to that and make sure that it was not issued. If anybody tries to remove the tag it can be traced with the help of location device.

Keywords: RFID, OPAC, Unauthorized user, tag, Reader.

INTRODUCTION

Radio Frequency Identification (RFID) systems are common and useful tools used in manufacturing, supply chain management, and inventory control. Industries as varied as microchip fabrication, automobile manufacturing, and even cattle herding have deployed RFID systems for automatic object identification. For over twenty years, consumer items have been identified with optical barcode. One familiar optical barcode is the Universal Product Code(UPC), designed in 1973[2] and found on many consumer products, More recently, RFID has made inroads into the consumer/object identification market. Silicon manufacturing advancements are making low-cost RFID, or "smart label" which seems to be an economical replacement for optical barcode.

ABOUT RFID TECHNOLOGY

System Components

An RFID system has three basic components, namely,

1. Radio Frequency (RF) tags or transponders that transmit the data to a reader .
2. RF readers or transceivers, devices which include an antenna to read and/or write data to RFID tags.
3. Communication system, a defined radio frequency and a protocol to transmit and receive data from tags.

Tag readers interrogate tags for their contents by broadcasting an RF signal. Tags respond by transmitting back resident data, typically including a unique serial number. RFID tags have several major advantages over optical barcode systems. Tag data may be read automatically, without line of sight, through non conducting materials such as paper or cardboard, at a rate of several hundred tags per second and from a range of several meters[1]. Since tags typically are silicon based microchips, functionality beyond simple identification may be incorporated into the design. This functionality might range from integrated sensors, to read/write storage, to support encryption and access control. Three example tags are shown in fig.1.

TYPES OF RFID SYSTEMS

One broad classification of RFID tags is whether they contain a microchip or not. "Chip" tags contain an integrated circuit chip, whereas "chip less" tags are less expensive to make and may store up to 24 bits of information-which provides enough memory for a company's internal use, such as on a ship floor or within a warehouse.

In order for a reader to identify all manufactured items, an RFID tag must have enough memory storage to hold ID number designed to identify a massive number of objects. And the reader must be able to read multiple tags within its range and in close proximity. Chip tag RFID systems enable data, such as a serial number or product code, to be stored and transmitted by portable tags to readers that process the data according to the needs of a particular application. Currently small chips are available which are able to store 96-bits of data – enough to include a manufacturer's name, a product name and one of trillions of unique numbers that can be assigned to products.

There are three types of tags: "read only", "write once read many (WORM)" and "read/write"[3]. They are "read only" if the identification is encoded at the time of manufacturing and not rewritable. "WORM" tags are programmable ones at the user end. But without the ability to rewrite them later while the "Read/write tags," have the ability to modify information.

The working of RFID systems and their features depend on the type of tag the system uses. There are two main types of RFID tags, namely, active or passive, which differ depending on whether they have their own power system.

Active RFID tags have both an on-tag power source and an active transmitter, offer superior performance. Because they are connected to their own battery, they can be read at a much higher range-from several kilometers away. But they are larger and more expensive and hence are suitable for manufacturing, such as tracking components on an assembly line, or for logistics – primarily where the tag device will be reused.

Passive tags have no power source and no on-tag transmitter, which gives them a range of less than 10 meters and make them sensitive to regulatory and environmental constraints. However, they have the most potential for lowest cost, making them suited for mass single-use applications.

RFID tags are interrogated by readers, which in turn are connected to a host computer. In a passive system the RFID reader transmits an energy field that "wakes up" the tag and powers its chip, enabling it to transmit or store data. Active tags may periodically transmit a signal, much like a lighthouse beacon, so that data may be captured by multiple readers distributed throughout a facility. The reader is equipped with antennas for sending and receiving signals a transceiver and a processor to decode data.

PROPOSED SYSTEM

In this paper a secure methodology for library management system using low cost RFID tags is proposed. RFID can be used for library circulation operations and theft detection systems. RFID-based systems move beyond security to become tracking systems that combine security with more efficient tracking of materials throughout the library, including easier and faster charge and discharge. The information contained on microchips in the tags affixed to library materials is read using radio frequency technology, regardless of item orientation or alignment

Privacy concerns associated with item-level tagging is another significant barrier to library use of RFID tags. The problem with today's library RFID system is that the tags contain static information that can be relatively easily read by unauthorized tag readers. Our paper emphasizes on this privacy concerns and proposes an alternative methodology to overcome the limitations of static information. The tag usage for the library books is shown in figure 2[7]. In the proposed method the information in the tag is dynamic.

COMPONENTS REQUIRED FOR THE PROPOSED RFID SYSTEM

The system has four components:

1) RFID tags that are electronically programmed with unique information. 2) Readers to query the tags 3) Antenna 4) Server to load the software that interfaces with the integrated library software.

WORKING OF THE PROPOSED RFID SYSTEM

Tags – The RFID tag can be fixed inside a book's back cover or directly onto CDs and videos. This tag is equipped with a programmable chip and an antenna. Each paper-thin tag contains an engraved antenna and a microchip with a capacity of at least 64 bits. "Read/write tags," are used in this system .

Readers – When a tag passes through the field, the information stored on the chip in the tag is interpreted by the reader and sent to the server, which, in turn, communicates with the integrated library system. RFID gate sensors (readers) at exits read the information on the tag(s) going by and communicate that information to a server. The server, after checking the circulation database, turns on an alarm if the material is not properly checked out. Readers in library are used at the following places in the library:

- Processing station: where object data (userid, volume no. etc of the books / magazines /CD's etc) is written to the tag.
- Circulation station: used for the issue and return of books / CDs etc.

- Check-in station: used for checking the books / CDs etc.
- Exit sensors: Used for verification of books/ CDs leaving the library.

Antenna – The antenna produces radio signals to activate the tag and read and write data to it. Antennas are the channels between the tag and the reader, which controls the system's data acquisitions and communication. The electromagnetic field produced by an antenna can be constantly present when multiple tags are expected continually. Antennas can be built into a doorframe to receive tag data from person's things passing through the door.

Server – The server is the communication gateway among the various components. It receives the information from one or more of the readers and exchanges information with the circulation database. Its software includes the SIP/SIP2 (Session Initiation Protocol), APIs (Applications Programming Interface) NCIP (National Circulation Interchange Protocol) or SLNP necessary to interface it with the integrated library software but no library vendor has yet fully implemented NCIP approved by NISO (Koppel, 2004). The server typically includes a transaction database so that reports can be produced.

SECURITY AND PRIVACY

RFID tags may pose security and privacy risks to both organization and individuals. Unprotected tags may have vulnerabilities to eavesdropping, traffic analysis, denial of service. Unauthorized readers may compromise privacy by accessing tags without adequate access control. Even if tags contents are protected, individuals may be tracked through predictable tag responses, essentially a traffic analysis attack violating location privacy. Another important privacy concern is tracking of individuals by RFID tags. A tag reader at a fixed location could track RFID labeled books carried by people passing by. To address the security risks of low cost RFID tags, passive tags will be used which provide simple identification functionality. Our tags contain a few thousand bits of storage and have an operating range of a few meters. Tag readers are assumed to have a secure connection to a backend database, although readers may only read tags from within the short tag operating range. A misplaced book or a tag sends a special alert to the reader, with the help of location device prompting the staff to rescue it. The tag consists of the following information:

LIMITATIONS OF RFID SYSTEMS

High cost – The major disadvantage of RFID technology is its cost.

Reader Collision – The signal from one reader can interfere with the signal from another where coverage overlaps. This is called reader collision. One way to avoid the problem is to use a technique called time division multiple access, or TDMA. In simple terms, the readers are instructed to read at different times, rather than both trying to read at the same time. This ensures that they don't interfere with each other. But it means any RFID tag in an area where two readers overlap will be read twice .

Tag collision – Another problem readers have is reading a lot of chips in the same field. Tag clash occurs when more than one chip reflects back a signal at the same time, confusing the reader. Different vendors have developed different systems for having the tags respond to the reader one at a time. Since they can be read in milliseconds, it appears that all the tags are being read simultaneously.

Lack of Standard – The tags used by library RFID vendors are not compatible even when they conform to the same standards because the current standards only seek electronic compatibility between tags and readers. The pattern of encoding information and the software that processes the information differs from vendor to vendor, therefore, a change from one vendor's system to the other would require retagging all items or modifying the software [4].

Best Practices for Libraries

As libraries are implementing RFID systems, it is important to develop best practices guidelines to utilize the technology in best way and to keep the privacy concern away. The following may be the best practices guidelines for library RFID use :

- The Library should be open about its use of RFID technology including providing publicly available documents stating the rational for using RFID, objectives of its use and associated policies and procedure and who to contact with questions.
- Signs should be pasted at all facilities using RFID. The signs should inform the public that RFID technology is in use, the types of usage and a statement of protection of privacy and how this technology differs from other information collection methods.
- Only authorized personnel should have access to the RFID system.
- No personal information should be stored on the RFID tag.
- Information describing the tagged item should be encrypted on the tag even if the data is limited to a serial number.
- No static information should be contained on the tag (bar code, manufacturer number) that can be read by unauthorized readers .
- All communication between tag and reader should be encrypted via a unique encryption key.
- All RFID readers in the library should be clearly marked.
- ISO 18000 mode-2 tags should be used rather than ISO 15693.

CONCLUSION

Radio Frequency Identification (RFID) Systems have been in use in libraries for book identification, for self checkout, for anti-theft control, for inventory control, and for the sorting and conveying of library books and audio visual materials. These applications can lead to significant savings in labor costs, enhance customer servicc, lowcr book thcft and providc a constant record update of media collections. In this paper, the technical features of a modern RFID system are described to provide a guideline for the evaluation of different systems. The most important result is that non-proprietary systems can be used for libraries today since the new generation of RFID chips with the ISO standard 15693 is available. With this technology, libraries are not dependent on one company for their lifeline.

REFERENCES

1. Boss. R. W. (2003). RFID technology for libraries [Monograph]. *Library Technology Reports*. November-December 2003.
2. Bibliotheca RFID Library Systems AG (2003) RFID Technology Overview. Retrieved from www.bibliotheca-rfid.com
3. Boss. R. W. PLA Tech Notes (May 14, 2004) RFID Technology for libraries. Retrieved from www.ala.org/ala/pla/plapubs/technotes/rfidtechnology.htm
4. http://libr.unl.edu:2000/LPP/shahid.html
5. Stephen A. Weis, Sanjay E. Sarma, Ronald L. Rivest and Daniel W. Engels "Security and Privacy Aspects of Low-Cost Radio Frequency Identification Systems".
6. Proposal for a Data Model " RFID Data Model for Libraries Working Group ", Affiliated to Danish Standard S24/u4, http://www.bs.dk/standards.
7. Ayre, Lori Bowen, The Galecia Group (August 2004) Position paper: RFID and libraries. Retrieved from www.galecia.com/weblog/mt/archives/cat_rfidandwireless.php

27

Application of Information Technology on Library Management

Jogdand Vinod Bhagwanrao

Documentlist, MIMSR Medical College Latur – 413512

INTRODUCTION

The objective of information technology is to provide better services to users by means of transmitting or messages in the form of written or printed records, electronic or any other medium. Information Technology plays an important role in information handling i.e. reeducation in computing time, capabilities resource sharing. Economic storage capacity of files on various mediums like discs, tapes etc.

This era is being recognized by terms and phrases such as 'Information Age', 'Wired Society', 'Global Age', 'Information Superhighway', 'Invisible Colleges', 'Technical Gatekeepers' all of which have implications on the functions and services of the library. The storage and retrieval of information taken various forms and formats like on-line databases, microfilm/fiche, telecommunications utilities, videotext etc. Information technology tools have changed the way libraries function. From electronic resource management to digital integration, license information to automation, recent examples what IT is essential for staying in sync with the best library practices in the world. In the IT ironment libraries would discover that 'Libraries without Walls' are actually only libraries with new alls – technologically bounded, legally restricted and administratively hamstrung.

IMPACT OF IT

Information Technology (IT) has affected and impacted the library services in many ways. In the under science, it has resulted in.

Automation of House-keeping Function

1. Acquisition
2. Cataloguing
3. Circulation
4. Serial Control

Library Services

1. Current Awareness Service
2. Selective Dissemination of information
3. Retrospective searches
4. Reference service
5. Interlibrary loan service
6. Document Delivery Service

IMPLICATION OF LIBRARY MANAGEMENT

The Major of application of IT on library management are that it leads to introduction of new services & systems for which LICs must have proper infrastructure.

IMPLICATION ON COLLECTION

Libraries are shifting from "Store house model" to "gateway

model" (Line, 1996) as future libraries will be providing access rather than ownership of collection.

It is evident that most of the documents are available in digital format.

IMPLICATIONS ON SERVICES

1. E-mail.
2. E-Shopping & e-ordering (e-commerce)
3. E-journals
4. Compact storage
5. OPAC
6. E-conferencing
7. Provision of CAS & SDI service
8. Resource sharing
9. Searching on-line database
10. Library resources at the doorsteps of users (with internet, intranet & extranet facility)

Implications on Library building

Financial implications

Implications on Manpower

Impact of IT on Library Management

Acceleration – Instant access to information, speed of computer.

Accuracy – Information manipulated or stored is accurate, require less Checking.

Amplification – Technology allows us to store & access more information. E.g. Engineering Index LISA

Archiving & Bibliographic Control – UBC exhaustive search is possible, can access than owning document.

Cost effective – Cost of machine are coming down. Printed book or Jr. is expensive but information stored on CD or website is cheaper.

Currency – retrieves nascent information as soon as it is published without time lag .

Decentralization – Decentralizatised input (INIS)

Centralized processing

Distributed output.

New Service (Products) – Mainpulation of statistics.

Current Addition list.

Current Awareness service

Documentation service.

Referral Service.

CONCLUSION

Although the new development in information technology are challenging, even overwhelming, the real challenges that we face are not technical in nature. Instead it is the need to imagine and implement change that will translate traditional values into the networked and electronic information in future.

It cuts across all sectors of the budget and it must reflect the recurring needs and long-term expenditures required to keep up to date. Otherwise hardware will become outdated, software obsolete, the librarians here is to retain the image of the library by using innovative information technology wisely and carefully. Librarians cannot become so carried away by information technologies that they are far ahead of their users. That is another good way to lose users. Librarians must remember the influence that changing generations will have on library services.

REFERENCES

- **Adams, Roy J. (1986).** *Information Technology and Libraries : a Future for Academic Libraries. Kent: Croom Helm. (Chapter : Staffing Requirments, 144-160)*
- **Balakrishana, N.** (1996) Impact of Information Technology on Library Science. In. Malwad, N.M.:
- **Rajashekhar, T.B.: Ravichandra Rao, I.K. :** Satyanarayana, N.V. (Eds.)

Digital Libraries : dynamic storehouse of digitalized information New Delhi: New Age International, 192-206.

- **Joshi Neha**, Conference paper on impact of IT on Library Management.
- **Vaishnav A. A.** Conference on impact of IT on Library Management.

29

Application of It on Library Science

More Balaji Kondibarao
bkmore.lib@gmail.com

ABSTRACT

New Technological development has brought a dramatic change in every field, and library science is not exception to it. Information technology impacted positively on library and information system and services they provide for users. This paper highlights on use of information technology in library science. It's areas its, importance.

Keywords **:** Information Technology, Reprographic Technology, Computer Technology, Telecommunication Technology.

INTRODUCTION

Today, we are living in the age of information . A large amount of information is being generated every movement. The ability to collect, store and disseminate this large amount of information needs application of new technologies for the re-arrange, select, marshal and transform of the information at phenomenal speed.

Information technology play very vital role in library science. For collection, storage, organization, processing, analysis of information. Use of information technology has great relevance in the context of forth law of library science "Save the time of the reader/staff " In which Ranganathan recognized the objective relating to the internal efficiency of the library.

DEFINITION OF INFORMATION TECHNOLOGY (IT)

Information Technology this concepts define as follows :

"The acquisition, Processing, Storage, & dissemination of vocal, pictorial, textual & theoretical information by a microelectronic-based combination of compute ring & telecommunication". - Rowely

"Development of information sources handled by computer & communicated by electronic channels, databases can thus be accessed by telephone & television links and computer put can be transmitted in an electronic format directly to a remote receiver." Harrod's Glossary

Nature Of Information Technology (IT)

In Library science or in library information technology used as various way these ways are as follows :

REPROGRAPHIC TECHNOLOGY

'Repro' means to rewrite or to reproduce & 'graphy' means printed or written matter. Therefore, Reprography reproductions of printed matter, Broadly, the various methods of reprography can be grouped under three or headings, according to basic process principles involved, they are :

Photographic methods (light sensitive)

Thermo graphic method (heat sensitive)

Electrostatic methods (charge sensitive)

COMPUTER TECHNOLOGY

Technology which accepts voice, pictures, text, symbols,

numbers, alphabets, etc. as input; process large of data & gives meaningful output.

Components	Auxiliary storage devices
Hardware	Software
CPU	Operating system
Input Devices	System utility programmers
Output Devices	Application Packages.

TELECOMMUNICATION TECHNOLOGY

'Tele' means at distance.' Communication' means exchange of ideas. Telecommunication technology is transmission of information over long distance via cable or radio waves.

COMPONENTS

Transmitter	-	to send the information.
Receiver	-	to accept the information.
Transmission medium	-	through which message travels
Signals & Codes	-	which represent message.
Network Control	-	to ensure message gets to its destination.

Communication technology uses inter phase technology, viz. computer & communication technology. It uses integrated facility, known as communication which involves transmission of information from one computer to the other using telecommunication technology. Sending & receiving computers are connected with communication technology.

NETWORK

Interlinking of many computers, terminals, & other devices by telecommunication links, according to structured architecture & agreed protocol for communication.

COMPONENTS

The components of network are :

Hardware

Media – Co-axial cable, twisted copper wire.

Proccssors

Modem

Multiplexer-transmission of data.

Switch-connecting various telecommunication circuits.

Router-routes the single to its intended destination.

Hub-automates switching among parts to share resources

Gateway-connecting networkingusing different. Network architecture.

Software

1. Network O.S (Windows NT, Linux, FoxPro,)
2. Internet Explorer

Types

LAN, MAN, WAN

Internet

Connects Computers all over the globe

Uses TCP/IP Protocols.

To search a website, we must know its URL.

Uniform Resource Locator (URL) provides address of information needed.

Used to identify & locate Internet resources.

URL consists of letters, numbers, punctuation marks & symbols.

Structure of URL is hierarchy, moves from left to right.

General form.

IMPORTANT OF INFORMATION TECHNOLOGY IN LIBRARY SCIENCE

1. Acceleration

2. Accuracy
3. Amplification
4. Cost effective :
5. Currency
6. Time Saving
7. Decentralization

CONCLUSION

In today application of information technology is the boon for library science.

REFERENCES

- **Harrod (1977).** The librarian's Glossary, London, Clarion Books.
- **Lancaster, F.W. (1982).** The future of library in the age of Telecommunication, In Changing Information.
- **Concepts & Technologies,** A reader for the professional Librarian. New York Knowledge Industry Publication. 145-164.
- **Line, M.B. (1996). Access vs. Ownership,** How real an Alternative in it? IFA Journal, 22-35-41
- **Rowley, Genefer (1988).** The Basics of information Technology. London. Clive Bingley.1
- **Vaishnav A. A.,** Conference paper on impact of IT on library management.

30

Application of IT in Library Science Field

Mrs.Shinde Bhavana Milind
(Librarian), Sinhgad College of Arts & Commerce, Pune
Mrs. Apte Shalaka Manoj
Sinhgad School of Business Studies, Pune

ABSTRACT

Libraries are experiencing enormous changes due to the application of Information Technology. The Library is a place where information is disseminated to needy clients in a user friendly environment. The era of IT has provided us various opportunities to access, store and retrieve desired information quickly and accurately. The application of computer for various library operations was a significant development in the later part of the last century. The Internet has provided universal access to information. Technological innovation has dramatically increased the rate of conversion of knowledge, information and data into electronic format. This paper discusses the use of IT in libraries to provide better services to the users with the help of library software, CD/DVDs, RFID application, digital libraries, institutional repositories, web OPAC and online database, e-books, e-journals, open access publishing etc. Thus the success of library and information science profession in future largely depends on how best they could make use of available information technology in performing their task and achieve productivity in obtaining set target.

INTRODUCTION

The information explosion is the rapid increase in the amount of published information in almost every field. As the amount of available data grows the problem of managing the information becomes more difficult. The era of Information Technology (IT) has provided us various opportunities to access, store and retrieve desired information quickly and accurately.

The technological improvement is changed the traditional library to digital library, library professionals to information professionals, collection development to content development, conventional education to web based education and information society to knowledge society.

IT AND LIBRARIES

In past the libraries which were considered only as the storehouses of knowledge, have got a new outlook in the modern IT era. The activities which were carried out manually in libraries with so much of pain and strain are being carried out smoothly with the help of IT with greater effectiveness. Library organization, administration and other technical processing have become easier and more quantum of work can be done in relaxed mood.

USE OF INFORMATION TECHNOLOGY IN LIBRARY

The use of IT in library consists of following areas of application.

1. Library Software

Library software is used to perform the various in-house library operations such as acquisition, processing, circulations, serial control management within less time and with less effort.

Library software enables to handle the extremely large collections with less manpower. Using the library software barcodes can be generated and barcodes are helpful in circulation section to save the time of users and which reduces the long queues of users at the circulation desk.

2. Institutional Repositories

Institutional Repositories (IR) are open access channels for collecting, preserving and disseminating the scholarly research in digit form i.e. IR are digital archives created by the faculty, staff and students of an institution or group of institutions. These digital archives are accessible by the users of both within and outside the institution. IR includes various types of publications, such as pre-prints and post prints of journal articles, conference papers, research reports, theses, dissertations, seminar presentations, working papers, and other scholarly items. The concept of IR and open access is needed due to the shrinking budgets and increasing cost of reading material. Thus this concept of open access and IR has evolved to find the solutions. Thus libraries have to adopt the new technology to provide the service to the users.

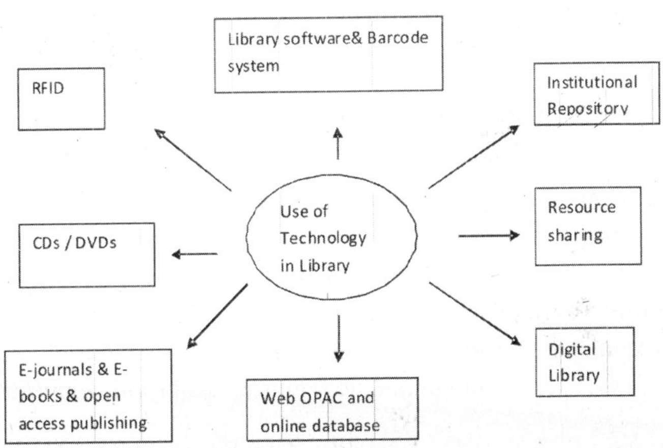

3. Resource Sharing:

Information explosion, paucity of financial resources, variety of information requirements of the users and problem of space necessitated the libraries and information centers to go for resource sharing through library network. Some of the examples of library networks are-i) Developing Library Network (DELNET),New Delhi, ii) Information and Library Network (INFLIBNET) , Ahmadabad, iii) Calcutta Library Network (CALIBNET), Calcutta, etc. which provides information resources to its clients through OPAC, database, document delivery and other network based information services.

4. Digital Libraries

Digital library is a library in which collections are stored in digital formats and accessible by computers. The digital content may be stored locally or accessed remotely via computer networks. A digital library is a type of information retrieved system. It is also a series of activities that brings together collections, services and people in support of the full life cycle of creation, dissemination, use and presentation of data, information and knowledge. It has expansive and accurate system of searching with large volumes of text, images and audio-video resources. Digital libraries do not need physical space to build collection and it can be accessed from anywhere, any time.

5. OPAC and E-databases

OPAC-Online Public Access Catalog-OPAC is an online database of materials held by a library or group of libraries.

Web OPAC is a powerful search engine for finding any cataloguing information from LibSys bibliographic database on-line.

E-databases

An e-database is an organized collection of information, of a particular subject or multidisciplinary subject areas. The information of an e-database can be searched and retrieved electronically. Contents include journal articles, newspaper articles, book reviews and conference proceedings, etc.e-databases usually updated on a daily, weekly, monthly or quarterly basis. Full text databases contain the whole content of an article such as citation information, text, illustrations, diagrams and tables. Bibliographic databases only contain citation information of an article, such as author name, journal title, publication date and page numbers.

We can only search for journal title in the Library Catalogue, but not the title or author of individual articles so e-database is extremely useful when you want to find articles on particular topics.

6. E-books

An electronic book is a text and image-based publication in digital form produced on, published by and readable on computers, other digital devices. e-books are usually read on dedicated hardware devices known as e-Readers or e-book devices. Personal computers and some cell phones can also be used to read e-books.

E-books are preferred by the users for their features like portability, upgradeability, note making, citation, changeable font size, references, links to other relevant sites, searching, etc.E-books can be transferred from library catalogue to users e-book readers for a fixed loan period and after which it is automatically taken back. An e-book can be offered indefinitely, without ever going "out of print".

In the space that a comparably sized print book takes up, an e-reader can potentially contain thousands of e-books, limited only by its memory capacity. If space is considered e-books collection takes up little room and weight.

7. E-journals

An article or complete journal available fully electronically via a web-site on the internet. They are specialized form of electronic document. They have the purpose of providing material for academic research and study and they are formatted approximately like journal articles in traditional printed journals.

E-journals facilitate documentation in many ways. They help for getting the most recent publications even before they are published in hard copy. The libraries can subscribe the journals online and get their log in details and upload in their local server. The e-journals provide closer link with a wider variety of publicizing and publishing by bringing informal and supplementary information into the closer proximity with formal, peer-viewed material.

8. Open Access Publishing

Open Access Journals are mostly used by researchers for their reference compared with other media. This also helps the researcher to find journal articles in his subject irrespective of their subscription. This helps libraries tackle the problems of small budget.

9. CDS/DVDS

Libraries use CD-ROMs in order to access large collections. Some CD-ROM indexes used by libraries are Reader's Guide to Periodical Literature, Books in Print , ProQuest's Periodical Abstracts and Academic Search or Alternative Press Index. Libraries could also purchase CD-ROM reference materials, which contain videos, animation, pictures and sound clips.

10. RFID-Radio Frequency Identifier

RFID has a tag which itself consists of a computer chip and an antenna, often printed on paper or some flexible medium. In short, RFID is like a barcode but is read with an electromagnetic field rather than by a laser beam. It is an advanced technology compared to barcode. It does not have to be visible to be read; instead it can be read even when it is embedded in an item such as cardboard cover of the book. It can also carry more complex message than a barcode which is limited to identification number.

The chip has the potential to carry not only the item number used by a library but also information such as the title of the book, it's call number etc. In the libraries RFID is mainly used to protect the library stock from theft.

CONCLUSION

The advent of Information Technology has paved the way of reducing the size of libraries from biggest to very small. In fact modern libraries are moving towards smaller and smaller but rich potential of information. This smallness of libraries is due to the digitization of information, has outcome a number of problems faced by traditional libraries since long. Providing right information to right user at the right time is an aim of any modern library .The success can be achieved with application of IT in libraries.

REFERENCES

1. Gardiner, Eileen and Ronald G.Musto."The Electronic Book." In Suarez, Michael Felix, and H.R. Waoudhuysen. The Oxford Companion to the Book.Oxford: Oxford University Press, 2010, p164
2. "E-books and their future in Academic Libraries", Lucia Snowhill,http://www.dlib/july01/snowhill/07snowhill.html
3. P.P.Singh Ed. And Sandhir Sharma Ed.,"E-Publishing: concepts and Practical Approaches", 2004
4. Budapest Open Access Initiative (2002),Open Society Institute, http://www.soros.org/openaccess.
5. Johnston, Colin. Electronic technology and its impact on libraries. Journal of Librarianship and Information Science.

LIBRARY MANAGEMENT

31

Library Management

Yallamma. T. Battase

Librarian Gupta College,Bangalore-560085

Mr. Anil Dhutraj

Librarian, Rohidas Patil Inst. of Management Studies Bhayandar, Mumbai

Mr. Karabasappa Kattimani

Librarian, G.S.S. Institute of Technology, Bangalore

ABSTRACT

Library management is defined as the process of coordinating total resources of an organization towards the accomplishment of desired goals of that organization through the execution of a group of inter related function such as planning, organizing, staffing, directing and controlling. Library is a non-profit making institution so it is necessary that finances by properly managed. General principles of management are applicable to library management. Library is building in which collections of books, tapes, news papers, etc, are kept for people read, study or borrow. It can be a personal collection of books, CD, etc, A Library can be a rental library i.e, a commercial establishment which is lending books for a fixed charge. It has a collection of manuscripts, publications and other materials for reading, study of reference. The main function of the library is collection, preservation and dissemination of knowledge to all. For this purpose a librarian is appointed. He is the one who is trained in library science and is enjoyed in library service. He is an officer in charge of a library. Then next step is of issuing a card by a circulating library to individuals entitling them to borrow books and sometimes constraining a record of the dates that book was borrowed and returned. It is also called borrower's card. And for all this, it ahs become necessary that every institution must have someone who makes things go well, which is called as management.

INTRODUCTION

Library is regarded as the brain of any institute; many institutes understand the importance of the library to the growth of the institute and their esteem users (students). LMS support the general requirement of the library like acquisition, cataloguing, circulation. Library project system that offers many flexible and convenient features, allowing librarians and library users to maximize time and efficiency. Library System gives the all detailed information about students, staff and books. It will track on the how many books available in library and books issued to the students. It shows popular book among the students. It will provide book lost in library. It keeps the record of the suppliers and book binders. It generates MIS reports for management.

Library Management System has been designed to automate, manage and look after the over-all processing of even very large-scale libraries. LMS is capable of managing Book Issues, Returns, Magazine/Newspaper Subscriptions, Calculating/Managing Fine and Balances of payments due from Members, generating various Reports for Record-Keeping and Review purposes, according to end user requirements.

More over LMS is fully compatible with Bar Code based management. Use of Bar Codes for Library Management eases the everyday tasks of big Libraries, where the No. of transactions exceed several thousands in number. Moreover, the LMS can work even without Bar Codes seamlessly. The Bar-Code generation and printing process is a Built-In feature of LMS. Librarians play a key role in creating an engaging learning and discovery environment for K-12 students. Today's school librarians need to be tech-savvy and intuitive about the learning styles and needs of each student. Besides managing administrative tasks, there is also a growing need for school librarians to collaborate more closely with classroom teachers in driving student achievement and helping students develop critical thinking, problem-solving and information search skills. Hence using Library management system helps librarians to perform the above tasks efficiently.

LIBRARY MANAGEMENT MEANING

Library management means managing all the happenings of the Library. Book transactions including Book Registration, Students Registration, Book Issuing, Current Status of a particular books etc. can be very easily handled by this module.

OPEN SOURCE LIBRARY MANAGEMENT SYSTEMS

There are already over 20 open source LMS projects of varying sizes visible through Source Forge. It is not uncommon for OSS projects to last only a few years and falter, either because of lack of ongoing patronage or lack of take-up. Projects that are clearly moribund or have no current installed base are not evaluated here.

The seven LMSs selected for analysis.

- Emilda—a small open source project with an attractive interface and a good installed base in small libraries;
- Evergreen—a more recent OSS with a good installed base and strong 'hype' in blogs;
- Gnuteca—a Brazilian OSS with strong installed base in non-English speaking countries;
- Koha--the oldest open source LMS, with a strong installed base;

- **OpenBiblio**—a system popular in small libraries, with simple installation and an effective presentation;
- **PhpMyLibrary**—developed in the Philippines and released not long after Koha, championing the use of MARC to facilitate adoption, and;
- **PMB** a French OSS with a strong installed base in Europe.

Although there is a range of open source licensing approaches, the popularly adopted LMSs examined here all use the GNU General Public License. Drummond provides a good review of alternative approaches to open source licensing. Other projects, such as UNESCO's WEBLIS LMS, are provided as freeware. A Koha offshoot called Learning Access ILS (http://www.learningaccess.org/tools/ ils.php), much discussed in several open source blogs, has not yet been released to open source. While these systems may well have strong functional merit, they provide no visibility in their development processes.

LIBRARY SYSTEM ANALYSIS

Due to the Expensive nature of the functions of library, there are two types of systems, i.e.,

1. Data processing system, and
2. Information system but specifically a library system mainly has 6 types of subsystems, which include the attributes of both the above systems also.

   These six subsystems are as follows:

- Acquisition subsystem
- Book circulation subsystem
- Administrative subsystem
- Cataloging subsystem
- Reference subsystem
- Serial control subsystem

Hence, the functions of libraries are analysis and coordinated by above six basic subsystems in which subsystems ate connected to each other, whose interconnected functions and relations are clear, and as a result of which these obtain pre determined objectives. In this way we can say that library is that system in which basic departmental limits remain present and there is no cause to artificial decentralization.

TYPES OF RECORDS MANAGEMENT SYSTEMS

Records management is an administrative function that maintains the records of an organization. It includes the management of records through retention policies, classification, storage, preservation and destruction. A record can be tangible, such as paper and microfilm, or simply consist of digital information stored electronically. Most modern organizations store the bulk of their records in digital form.

Document Management System – A document management system (DMS) promotes creating, finding and sharing information. A DMS usually takes the form of business software. It assists in organizing and disseminating the organizational knowledge base. A DMS features easy access to relevant data and facilitates information mining. It often includes security features. Security is important to maintain an organization's critical data and business secrets. Security features also serve to protect personal user information and customer data.

Content Management System – A content management system consists of the rules, procedures and processes used to manage work flow for an organization. A benefit of a CMS is the ability of end users to collaborate on document creation and revision. Organizations use CMSs as centralized data storage. The centralized access to documents provides a platform for end users to control, revise, publish and add commentary. A CMS also facilitates communication between users.

Library Management System – A library management system (LMS) is an enterprise resource planning system for a library. It is used to track individual items and patron accounts, and to monitor a library's entire collection. The LMS consists of a centralized database and a method for the patrons and staff to interact with the system. Library staff has access to functionality that includes acquisitions, cataloging and circulation. Serial subscriptions are also tracked from the LMS.

Digital Imaging System – Digital imaging systems (DIS) give organizations the ability to capture, store and distribute an enormous number of records over electronic networks. In the past, businesses relied on paper and microfilm for storage. A DIS speeds the search and retrieval process for documents and information. Organizations can save considerable storage space because of the decrease in the need for filing cabinets and other storage devices. Online dissemination of data and the ability to integrate with other information management systems is the main benefit of a DIS.

CONCLUSION

In a traditional sense, a library is a large collection of books or other reading material, and can refer to the place in which the collection is housed. Today, the term can refer to any collection, including digital sources, resources, and services. The collections can be of print, audio, and visual materials in numerous formats, including maps, prints, documents, microform (microfilm/ microfiche), CDs, cassettes, videotapes, DVDs, video games, e-books, audio books and many other electronic resources.

Only basic knowledge of computers is required for operation of Library Management System. As it has user-friendly application interface. Library Management System is Customizable and User Configurable. An inbuilt Settings module makes Library Management System flexibility to cater to diverse organizational needs. There are already over 20 open source LMS projects of varying sizes visible through Source Forge. It is not uncommon for OSS projects to last only a few years and falter, either because of lack of ongoing patronage or lack of take-up. While these systems may well have strong functional merit, they provide no visibility in their development processes.

REFERENCE

- Cohen, L.B. (2007). "A Manifesto for our time". American Libraries 38: 47–9.
- Denslaw, Debra. (2005). "Innovate to Motivate: The Relationship Between Great Managers and Great Employees." Trends, 16(2), 4-6.
- Harris, Michael H. (1984). The History of Libraries in the Western World. London: Scarecrow Press. ISBN 0810816660.
- Mathews, Virginia H. 2004. Libraries, citizens & advocacy: the lasting effects of two White House Conferences on Library and Information Services. [Washington, D.C.?]: White House Conference on Libraries and Information Services Taskforce.
- McCook, Kathleen de la Peña (2011). Introduction to Public Librarianship, pp. 75-99. ISBN 978-1-55570-697-5.
- Orenstein, David. (2003). "Fair Pay Is an Issue for Managers, Too." Library Journal, 128(6), 45.
- Paula D. Watson, "Founding Mothers: The Contribution of Woman's Organizations to Public Library Development in the United States", Library Quarterly, Vol. 64, Issue 3, 1994, p.236
- Teva Scheer, "The "Praxis" Side of the Equation: Club Women and American Public Administration", Administrative Theory & Praxis, Vol. 24, Issue 3, 2002, p.525
- The American International Encyclopedia, J. J. Little & Ives, New York 1954, Volume IX

32

Study of E-Manuscripts Available at Indira Gandhi National Centre for the Arts (IGNCA)

Dr. Mangala A. Hirwade
Associate Professor, Dept. of LIS, RTMNU, Nagpur

Mrs. Sangita R. Chore
Librarian, Br. Sheshrao Wankhede Arts & Comm. College, Khaperkheda

ABSTRACT

The glorious past of Indian culture lies in the ancient manuscripts. These are the basic historical evidence and have great research value. It is estimated that India possesses more than five million manuscripts, making her the largest repository of manuscript wealth in the world. Though our ancestors had tried to preserve these manuscripts, thousands of such valued unpublished Indian manuscripts on varied subjects are lying scattered or fragmented in India and foreign collections and some of these are no longer accessible to research scholars. This invaluable and unique pool of knowledge is under threat and manuscripts are disappearing at an alarming rate. To achieve various challenges Indian National Manuscripts Library at IGNCA has been proposed. With all manuscript resources compiled at IGNCA under Kala Nidhi and NMM projects, a centralized repository of manuscripts will be available to the users worldwide. The National Manuscript Library is being designed to inspire research on and ensure recycling of the knowledge content in the manuscripts. The Indira Gandhi National Centre for the Arts (IGNCA) was established in 1987 as an autonomous institution under the Ministry of Culture, as a centre for research, academic pursuit and dissemination in the field of the arts. The IGNCA has six functional units - Kala Nidhi, Kala Kosa, Janapada Sampada, Kaladarsana, Cultural Informatics ,and Sutradhara . Kala Nidhi a National Information System and Data Bank, consists of the reference library of print collections, a large library of Microfilms/Microfiches, collection of slides, cultural archives and photo documentation in the disciplines of Arts and Archaeology

***Keywords*:** Manuscripts, e-manuscripts, Indira Gandhi National Centre for the Arts (IGNCA)

INTRODUCTION

The Indira Gandhi National Centre for the Arts (IGNCA) was established in 1987 as an autonomous institution under the Ministry of Culture, as a centre for research, academic pursuit and dissemination in the field of the arts. The Arts' encompass a wide range of subjects - from archaeology and anthropology to the visual and performing arts, enveloping them in a complementary and non-demarcated vision. In its functioning, the IGNCA has met its mandate and continues to work in this direction. The Indira Gandhi National Centre for the Arts is visualized as a centre encompassing the study and experience of all the arts –each form with its own integrity, yet within a dimension of mutual interdependence, interrelated with nature, social structure and cosmology.

The IGNCA has six functional units – Kala Nidhi, Kala Kosa, Janapada Sampada, Kaladarsana, Cultural Informatics, and Sutradhara. Kala Nidhi a National Information System and Data Bank, consists of the reference library of print collections, a large library of Microfilms/Microfiches, collection of slides, cultural archives and photo documentation in the disciplines of Arts and Archaeology Recognizing the need to encompass and preserve this knowledge resource and to make these accessible to scholars and researchers, Indira Gandhi National Centre for the Arts (IGNCA) initiated the most important manuscript-microfilming programme in 1989. It has approached many of the private and public institutions and individuals who are in possession of valuable manuscripts preferably in Sanskrit Language and has signed Memorandum of Understanding with each of them for microfilming of their manuscripts.

OBJECTIVES

The main objectives of this paper are

- To Study e-manuscripts collection in microfilm / microfische ,
- To study state wise and organization wise catalogue of manuscripts available at the IGNCA,
- To discuss Material wise collection at IGNCA
- To trace Language/ Script wise collection.

WHAT IS A MANUSCRIPT?

Manuscript means something that is hand written. Here the term manuscript is related to antiquity not necessarily means the write up submitted by an author to a publisher. The Antiquities and Art Treasures Act, 1972 lays down the legal framework for custody of manuscripts. Antiquities, defined under the Act include "any manuscript, record or other document which is of scientific, historical, literary or aesthetic value and which has been in existence for not less than seventy-five years." If this definition is taken into consideration in phase value, a manuscript means

- a hand written document
- which has scientific, historical, literary or aesthetic value and
- which is at least seventy-five year old.

INDIAN NATIONAL MANUSCRIPTS LIBRARY AT IGNCA

To achieve various challenges as mentioned above Indian National Manuscripts Library at IGNCA has been proposed. With all manuscript resources compiled at IGNCA under Kala Nidhi and NMM projects, a centralized repository of manuscripts will be available to the users worldwide. This is going to the first such library in the world, and of course the foremost, to among all other institutions to fulfill the twin objectives of preservation and access to Indian manuscripts. The National Manuscript Library is being designed to inspire research on and ensure recycling of the knowledge content in the manuscripts. Indeed a revolutionary concept.

KALA NIDHI

This information System and Data Bank will serve as a major resource centre for research in humanities, in the arts, in the disciplines of Archaeology, Anthropology, History, Philosophy, Literature, Language, Arts, and Crafts etc.

Branches of Kala Nidhi

- Reference Library
- Cultural Archive
- Reprography Unit
- Slide Unit
- Media Production Unit
- Photography Unit
- Conservation Unit

The reference library of IGNCA has a large collection in the broad areas of humanities and the arts. It constitutes books, reprographics of several folios of unpublished Sanskrit, Pali, Persian and Arabic manuscripts in microfilm and microfiche, photographs and slides.

Reprography Unit

A unique feature of the Reprography unit of the Kalanidhi is the reprographic compilation of unpublished manuscripts in Indian and foreign collections from private and public libraries. A pioneering attempt has been made to bring under one roof primary sources of the Indian tradition lying scattered, fragmented, inaccessible or worse, in danger of extinction. At present the library contains more than ten millions folios of unpublished Sanskrit, Pali, Persian and Arabic manuscripts. Total 20,000 microfilm rolls (approx.) containing 2.5 lacs mss. have been generated so far.

ACCESS TO IGNCA MANUSCRIPTS COLLECTION

Scholars and researchers can access the microfilm/ microfiche collection at the IGNCA and they can also obtain copies, subject to copyright restrictions, and indeed the conditions spelt out in the MoU signed between IGNCA and concerned manuscript Library. As a general practice, one needs to seek permission of concerned library to obtain a copy of the manuscript from IGNCA Collection. Copies are being made available in digital / microfilm / print formats on charge basis. The consultation to all above manuscripts at IGNCA Reference Library is open to all without any charges. Online catalogue of these manuscripts in MARC 21 will be made available soon.

NATIONAL MISSION FOR MANUSCRIPTS, IGNCA, NEW DELHI

The National Mission for Manuscripts (NMM) is the first consolidated national effort for reclaiming India's inheritance of knowledge contained in the vast treasure of manuscripts. The Mission was established in 2003 by the Ministry of Tourism and Culture with Indira Gandhi National Centre for the Arts as it's nodal

The major objectives of the Mission are

- Survey, document and catalogue Indian manuscripts, in India and abroad, and compile a National Database
- Facilitate conservation and preservation of manuscripts through training, awareness building and financial support
- Provide ready access to these manuscripts through digitization and publication
- Promote scholarship and research in the study of Indian languages and manuscript logy
- Set up a National Manuscripts Library at the Indira Gandhi National Centre for the Arts, New Delhi

The National Mission for Manuscripts engaged itself with the detailed documentation of the manuscripts in India, by creating a National Catalogue of Manuscripts known as Kritisampada the National Database of Manuscripts provides information of manuscripts from institutions – religious, cultural and educational, as well as private collections across the country, and also from Indian collections abroad.

MANUSCRIPTS COLLECTION IN MICROFILM / MICROFISCHE

Kala Nidhi Reprography Unit has initiated a manuscript-microfilming programme a few years back. The IGNCA has approached many of the private and public institutions and individuals who are in possession of valuable manuscripts, preferably in Sanskrit, and has signed a Memorandum of Understanding with each of them for microfilming their manuscripts. So far the Reprography Unit has microfilmed over 2.78 lakh manuscripts in 21506 microfilm rolls. All the rolls have been duplicated, digitized and catalogued.

CONCLUSION

India is the largest repository of manuscript wealth in the world which needs to be preserved and provided access to the national mission for manuscripts is a challenging task. It opens a door to an engagement with the preservation of our knowledge and heritage. The mission aims to locate, catalogue and preserved India's manuscripts and also to enhance access, spread awareness and encourage their use for educational and research purposes. It provided opportunity for all governments at Central and State levels, cultural and knowledge institutions in the government and private sector and all concerned citizens to come together to make it realize its objectives.

REFERENCES

- Gaur, Ramesh C.,2009 Preservation and Access to Indian Manuscripts : A Knowledge Base of Indian Cultural Heritage Resources for Academic Libraries, http://crl.du.ac.in/ical09/papers/index_files/ical-14_227_489_2_RV.pdf [Accessed 2/08/2011].
- Gopalkrishnan, Manuscripts and IndianKnowledge System: The past Contextualizing
- Kumar S and Shah, Leena "Digital Preservation of Manuscripts : A Case Study",http://ir.inflibnet. ac.in: 8080/ jspui/bitstream/ 1944/419/ 1/ 04Planner_5.pdf (acessed 02/7 2011).
- Mazumdar Nirmal Ranjan,2009. Digital Preservation of Rare Manuscripts in Assam. [online] Available at: http://www.inflibnet.ac.in/caliber2009/ CaliberPDF/2.pdf [Accessed on 18/07/2011].
- National Mission of Manuscripts.2003. [online] Available at: www.namami.nic.in [Accessed 01/08/2011].Prasad, Panda Ganesh. Dec 2006. *Kritisampada*: The National Database of Manuscript

33

Management in Academic Libraries

Mr. Kuldeep P.Pawar

Librarian, Pratishthan College, Paithan, Dist-Aurangabad

Dr. Shamkant Deshmukh

Librarian, Nutan Maratha college, Jalgaon

Mr. Nandkishor B. Gosvi

Librarian, Shatabdi Institute of engineering, agaskhind , Nashik

ABSTRACT

Total quality management is the need of today's world in every industry. It may be manufacturing industry or it may manufacturing industry or it may be service industry like banking, hoteling, or library etc. Total quality management in libraries is a step to advancement. TQM reduces critical procedures. This paper discusses steps required to implement TQM in libraries, Benefits to Libraries and Barriers to implement TQM in libraries. This paper helps to researchers to understand various aspects of TQM implementation in Library.

Keywords : Orientation, Empowerment, tolerance

INTRODUCTION

TQM

Total Quality Management (TQM) programs in an attempt to retain or regain competitiveness in order to achieve customer satisfaction in the face of increasing competition from around the world in this era of globalization. TQM is an integrative philosophy of management for continuously improving the quality of processes.TQM functions on the premise that the quality of the products and processes is the responsibility of everyone who is involved with the creation or consumption of the products or services offered by the organization. In other words, TQM capitalizes on the involvement of management, workforce, suppliers, and even customers, in order to meet or exceed customer expectations

TQM IN LIBRARIES

Among the service industries such as Airlines, Banks, Insurance companies, hotel, hospitality, Health care providers, Libraries are also going to adopt TQM practices in world. For a long time, Librarians feel themselves as keepers of knowledge rather than guide or provider of Information. The main aim of libraries is to satisfy the users, librarians often forget that they also a service provider to customers i.e. to Students and society. But today's libraries are pushed to a position where they have to provide quality services to its users, to justify their existence otherwise there are no footprints of old libraries. So, now libraries are also started adopting TQM practices following other kinds of service industries.

BENEFITS OF TQM TO LIBRARIES :

Particular	*Traditional Library*	*TQM oriented Library*
Stucture	Central	Distributed
Goals / Objectives	Short term	Long term
Backup	No	Yes

Tolerance of waste	Low	High
Fire fighting	No	Yes
Inspection	Severally	Oftenlly
Top-down hierarchy	Yes	NO
Isolation	Yes	No
Management	Custodian	Management By objective

POTENTIAL CHALLENGES TO IMPLEMENT TQM IN LIBRARIES

The implementation of TQM in library provides an opportunity to update and enhance the abilities of the staff to work efficiently and effectively; yet it is still not free from some of barriers.

I) Unavailability of sufficient funds

II) Physical factors

III) The Process Barrier

IV) The commitment Barrier

CONCLUSION

The success of TMQ is depends upon the factors like strategy, cooperation of staff, customers as well as funds. It is a process which focuses on understanding customer needs and improving customer's service and satisfaction. Goals of libraries must be strategic and long term. If preliminary objectives get fulfilled then try to change objective in the light of vision of the organization.The realities of the current library situation indicates that quality improvement is essential not only but for facing major changes and growth required for the libraries as well as customer satisfaction today and tomorrow

REFERENCES

- Butcher, K. S. (1993). Total quality management: The Oregon State University Library's experience. "Journal of Library Administration," 18(1/2), 45-56. (EJ 469 102)
- Deming, W. E. (1986). "Out of the crisis." Cambridge, MA: Massachusetts Institute of Technology, Center for Advanced Engineering Study.

- Jurow, S. & Barnard, S. B. (1993). Introduction: TQM fundamentals and overview of contents. "Journal of Library Administration," 18(1/2), 1-13. (EJ 469 099)
- Mackey, T. & Mackey, K. (1992). Think quality! The Deming approach does work in libraries. "Library Journal," 117(9), 57-61. (EJ 446 234)